In Spite of
OCEANS

In Spite of
OCEANS
MIGRANT VOICES

HUMA QURESHI

For Suffian

First published 2014

The History Press
The Mill, Brimscombe Port
Stroud, Gloucestershire, GL5 2QG
www.thehistorypress.co.uk

© Huma Qureshi, 2014

The right of Huma Qureshi to be identified as the Author
of this work has been asserted in accordance with the
Copyright, Designs and Patents Act 1988.

British Library Cataloguing in Publication Data.
A catalogue record for this book is available from the British Library.

ISBN 978 1 84588 818 3

Typesetting and origination by The History Press
Printed in Great Britain

Contents

In spite of the ocean that now separated her from her parents, she felt closer to them, but she also felt free, for the first time in her life, of her family's weight.

Acknowledgements

My deepest gratitude to my publisher, Ronan Colgan, who read my writing and took a chance on me. Thank you, and everyone involved with the publication of this book at The History Press, for your patience and your confidence.

This book would never have been written were it not for the incredible individuals whose fascinating experiences inspired these stories. You shared with me your deepest emotions. I cannot thank you enough.

My heartfelt thanks to all those who helped with feedback on the early stages of this book. I am especially indebted to The Authors' Foundation for selecting *In Spite of Oceans* for the John C. Laurence Award.

My talented best friend and fellow writer agreed to be my first reader. Thank you, Karen Onojaife. You are especially golden to me.

I could not have written this book without the support of every single member of my Qureshi and Birch family. You gave me the time and space I needed to write. All of you have been wonderfully patient with me.

I particularly thank my parents. My father's memory lies somewhere in these pages. Amee, you remain an inspiration. Thank you for your unwavering belief in my many risk-taking leaps.

And also my brothers, Usman and Imran. Neither of you seem to think anything I write is bad and you both blow my trumpet for me at every opportunity in a way only big brothers can. I am one exceptionally and eternally grateful little sister. Saba, my sister-in-law, your infectious exuberance never fails to lift me. Thank you.

To my parents-in-law, I am humbled by your pride in me and I hope this book lives up to expectations.

And finally to Richard, who took care of our beautiful baby boy while I struggled with deadlines, self-doubt and writer's block. You held the three of us together when I needed it most, at the times when I thought I would never be able to finish this book. You steady me each time I falter and have taught me to be kinder to myself, in spite of it all. For that, I thank you, always.

Introduction

There is a framed black-and-white photograph that sits on the window sill of my childhood bedroom. It is of a woman I never knew. And yet there it is, in a place that I still call mine.

She has unlined almond eyes, thick heavy eyebrows and jet black hair parted deeply, held tight in a stiff, shiny wave fixed to the side as, I suppose, was the style. Her sari is pinned to her shoulder and she wears rings on every finger of her clasped hands, a few thin bangles clustered at her wrist. She is my mother's mother, my naani, my grandmother.

She is not a smiling grandma; rather, her expression is halfway between sad and serious as she stares into the camera, her lips pressed together. She gives nothing away.

All I have of my grandmother is this, this old photograph in my bedroom in the house where I grew up in the West Midlands. There are no family jewels that have been passed along, no heirlooms that have stood the test of time. Even if there had been, it is not likely they would have travelled this far. Not across countries, continents and oceans, not all the way to England and not to me.

My grandmother died a long time ago. She died in Pakistan, far away from where she was born in Uganda. My mother, the second-youngest child of seven, was 14 years old when my naani passed away.

I don't know much about my grandmother. Growing up, I never thought to ask. But now that I am older, now that I think about these things more, I wonder. I wonder about heritage and history and how this woman that stares at me like a stranger so blankly and, if I am altogether honest, sadly from behind a frame is in some way a part of me, if she is at all. Tell me, I think, looking at her photo. Tell me who you were.

More recently, I have asked my mother about my naani, from time to time. But what she remembers of that short period in her life when she, too, had a mother is blurry now.

This is what happens when your roots are rambling, overgrown from one country to the other in a tangled, wild nest that is home to more relatives than you ever really know. Time passes, memories mix facts with fiction and people forget how they got to where they are. My family history is not ordered, neat and tidy, logically flowing from one generation to the next. I cannot point at this name or that on an inked family tree and say 'Yes, he owned this land,' or 'He fought that war,' or 'She came from this place,' that I might then pick out on a map.

No, our story is not like that. My family history is the history of a family of immigrants. Many of my relatives, living or long gone, made their homes in different places starting first in pre-partition India and then in post-partition Pakistan, leaving a young country of unspoken promise to head further afield. One set of great-grandparents left to live in East Africa and work proudly for the British Empire. From there, one grandfather went to Saudi Arabia while the other engineered railways in the British Raj. Countless uncles and aunts forayed, one by one, out of Pakistan, followed by my own parents too, landing in England, where they stopped still; then cousins spiralling, now quickly and urgently, as fast as they can, to the Middle East, Australia and America. My big, extended family has spun like a spider's silk web everywhere for decades, delicate skeins of DNA held together across lands first in blunt, capitalised telegrams and papery aerogrammes, now in virtual messages that take merely seconds to send.

All of these people I am related to left the places they were born, the familiarity of language, of food and of the faces they loved, for something else. Some left in pursuit of what they thought would be better lives; others left for what they felt was duty. Many left to fulfil ambition which they would not in all their pragmatism dare call dreams.

Sometimes they struggled, sometimes it was too hard. Some returned to Pakistan permanently, to their homeland and their mother tongue, building new houses with foreign money and saying sadly with a smile, 'Well, we tried.' Sometimes they fell in love with their new surroundings. Some of them, like my parents, stayed in one place, raising children who spoke differently to them and whose references of childhood were so far removed from what they once knew. It was us, the children, who rooted them steadfast in humdrum suburban towns that became home. And so, as years passed, places like Pakistan for my father or Uganda for my mother faded further and further away.

I may not have made the journey my parents made, but it is because of them that I am here, an adopted Londoner now. The choices they made long before I was born determined who I was to be and the path I would take. My past, surely, explains my present.

This is the connection I have explored in all of the stories that follow. The stories are inspired by people I have met. Some of them left south Asia behind and have long since made Britain their home. Others are like me, born and raised in one place but with a heritage from afar.

The people behind these stories have shared fragments of their quiet histories with me and I have, at times, filled in the gaps between the pieces they provided using my imagination. At these times, I have envisaged scenes and asked myself to wonder how some moments may have been. All the while, the essence of these individual experiences has been preserved.

Every story is, in its own way, a story of a journey. Sometimes the journey is literal, moving across oceans. Other times it is intangible, a journey of understanding and, often, coming to terms with what some call circumstance and others call fate. Each of these stories explores, in its own way, the connection to a different land and a different time, place and culture somewhere on the Indian subcontinent. Sometimes that connection is cherished and celebrated. Other times it is severed abruptly with hurt and pain. In some cases, it is simply something that just cannot be shaken or thrown away, binding us against our will, or forever in the background, quietly humming. Sometimes the connection is strong and loud, other times it is vague, weak and fading. But no matter how subtle it is, it is always there, a reminder of the past forever present and the journeys we make to be who we are, where we are, today.

1

Learning to drive

Afra travels light. In her small suitcase, she carries only one simple sari, three long dresses, a cardigan and a few plain undergarments. In the inside pocket of her handbag, she keeps her passport and copies of her maths degree.

It is not much, for a young woman about to move countries. It is even less, for a bride. She does not mind. She does not care for her dowry, the heavy saris her mother gave her or the gold gifted to her by her in-laws.

'I will not need them,' she tells her mother and her mother-in-law when they try to give her ornate saris to carry, telling her a wife will need more than what she has packed. 'I will not need them where I am going.'

There is not much of her dowry left to take, in any case. Weeks after their wedding, she gave most of her trousseau away after Abbas told her she looked like a prostitute in the saris her mother had picked out for her in her favourite colour, the oranges of henna stains, and painstakingly folded into the wardrobe her father had bought for her to take to her new marital home. Her in-laws, new cousins and cousins' wives and aunts and women whose names she was yet to learn, bounded into her room, plucking free saris in varying shades of amber and ochre and autumn as if the rice harvest had come early to Sylhet this year.

'Take them,' Afra shrugged. 'Take them all.' As they helped themselves, they thought her a funny girl, to give her beautiful clothes away.

Later, Abbas threw the few things that were left into the courtyard in a drunken rage. Her clothes, the plain ones she had stitched herself; dinky pots of lurid make-up pastes given to her by her college friends; inexpensive but pretty little bracelets from her four younger sisters; her father's copy of Agatha Christie's *The Murder at the Vicarage* which he said she could keep; folders of maths notes from the degree she was studying for before the marriage proposal came. Abbas threw it all into the courtyard, storming like a hurricane towards her.

'I never wanted this! I never wanted you!' He jabbed his fingers towards her, pushed his face so close to hers she could smell his sour breath and see the spittle bubble on his cracked lips. The few things she had kept for herself lay ruined in a dirty heap in the middle of the courtyard. Afraid of her new husband to whom she had been married for less than a month, she turned and ran while her mother-in-law tried desperately to restrain her son. 'I never wanted her!' he screamed at his mother. 'I never wanted her! You did this!'

That was nearly a year ago. Afra has not seen Abbas since. After he threw her things into the courtyard, his brother hurriedly arranged for Abbas to go back to England, where he had been living before his wedding to Afra and where it had already been decided upon their brief engagement that she would join him.

'You go back and you make things better,' he told his younger brother. 'You make a living and you go back with her.'

Abbas left quickly but Afra did not go with him. In the first interview for her visa which her brother-in-law had arranged for her at the British High Commission in Dhaka, Afra told the commission officer in the privacy of the interview room that she did not need a visa after all.

'I am married to a stranger. I do not want to go to England with him. I want to stay in Bangladesh,' she said in her college-taught English, shunning the interpreter who looked on, stunned by this young woman who was not even trying to impress like all the others who came in nervous and polite, overdressed in smart shoes and starched clothes and desperate for the stamp on their passport that would let them leave for a new life.

The officer raised an eyebrow, nodded and said 'Very well'. Then he refused her application and wished her the best.

But now Afra is going. In her second visa interview she told the officer, a fair-haired Englishman named Mark, that she was ready to leave.

'I have heard a lot about England,' she said. 'I have heard I can get an education there. Here, I just do everything for everyone else. In England, perhaps I can stand up on my own two feet. I will work there. I will get a job. It is the only place where I can be free.'

The officer looked at her, this small, serious woman who, according to her passport, was only 19 years old.

He deliberated and then he said, 'No more questions.' Her passport was stamped immediately, and her small suitcase has been packed ever since.

Abbas is on his way back to Bangladesh from England for the first time since their marriage. He is coming to collect her. After six weeks, they will leave together. Her mother and her mother-in-law are proudly telling everyone, relieved at finally being able to say, 'He is coming for her, she will go with him. They will be happy in their lives together.'

Though Afra has had her suitcase packed, she is not excited like her mother. But she is ready to go. She is frustrated and bored, being a wife in Bangladesh to a man overseas, when all she really wants is a job, a purpose, something to call her own. Still, she does not know what they will do for money although she read in a letter to his mother that Abbas has a job as a waiter now at a friend's restaurant in a city called Durham. She does not know much about Durham. But the thought of moving to an unknown country and an unknown city does not scare her. She just wants to go.

Her father gives her a notebook. It is filled with neatly written phone numbers of uncles and aunts, who are not relatives but friends of her family settled in London. He tells her these friends will look after her no matter what she needs. This notebook and the copies she carries of her maths degree calm the few sparkling nerves she allows herself to feel. She is weary of Bangladesh and she wants to be free.

Afra was not told married life would be like this. She was told her husband was a straightforward man, an honest man, that is what her family said. She thought, at the very least, that he would speak to her kindly and that one day, perhaps, they might love each other. But it has not happened yet. For how could it? He has been away for so long.

Though her throat tightens when she thinks of parting from her father, she hopes the distance this new country will bring will separate her from the hurt that those around her brought to her, put upon her and bound her in. She hopes her hurt will scatter and then disappear, like the tear-shaped raindrops that fell so heavily the month she married.

When she was young, she had been promised much. First it was little things, a bike and new books. And then it was bigger things, an education and a job. Her father wanted it all for her, his eldest daughter whose name he called out first as soon as he got home. In his gestures and words, he promised her the world. He promised her a co-education at the college he went to, a modern life ahead of her of independence.

It was the late 1960s. It was East Pakistan. Afra's father was a liberal and he believed his little girl could grow up to be different to the women that had surrounded him all his life. He had seen first his sister, and then his own wife, limited by their basic primary school education, prepared only for marriage, housekeeping and nothing else. Afra would be different, he decided. He took her to the library, cycled with her on the back of his bike, talked to her about books, and other things she did not yet understand like politics and college courses even though she was still a child.

'One day,' he said proudly as she showed him her latest round-up of top marks from school, 'one day this daughter of mine will be so successful! She will drive a car, and I will sit at the back and she will take me around. Just watch!' Her mother shrieked in shame. No daughter of hers would ever drive a car, she retaliated.

But the dreams both Afra and her father had hoped for never came or if they did, they were quickly taken away. For a day she rode on a shiny new bike from her father before her mother replaced it with a sewing machine, declaring it a far better way for a teenage girl to pass her time. When her father brought home bundles of new books he thought would expand his daughter's young mind, her brother wrote his name in them instead.

Then in 1971 things changed. Her father, a customs officer for the government, grew terrified of the soldiers from West Pakistan who ruled violently in the streets. Twice they came for him. Twice he begged to be freed and then refused to speak of what had happened to him, shaking his head gravely instead, turning blankly away, unable to look into another person's eyes for too long. Brave men, liberal men like her father, lived in fear of a bloody civil war that threatened their everything.

Her mother made Afra stay home and indoors, away from the stories they heard of the rape of young girls, of torture, of beatings and kidnappings. Afra was only 10 years old when the war broke out but her mother, who was married herself at 11, insisted she be married quickly because five daughters in the house was a risk.

'Let her be protected in her husband's house. We cannot let her go out,' she urged in a whisper.

Her father grew quieter, his face worn and worried and resigned. He agreed.

'It is for the best, beti jaan,' he told Afra when he explained she could not return to school for a year.

Afra's mother looked every day for the red smudge of blood that would declare her daughter's readiness for marriage. But for two years it did not come, despite her prayers. When it finally did, the war was over and then all of a sudden, the rush of suitors did not stop. Their mothers and their sisters came to drink tea at their home and eat the snacks Afra had prepared. Some were families they already knew from Sylhet, others travelled from afar in serious search of a bride. Sometimes the prospective grooms came too. They were older than Afra and casually looked up from their china cups from time to time, watching her with an indifference which implied they were not there for her at all.

Afra did not have to resist being married all these years; her father did it for her. He enrolled her in the college he himself had attended, as he always said he would, and she was fast becoming a top maths student. Her tutor suggested finance as a career and her father approved. But he always left the house when the suitors and their families arrived, and later he argued about it with her mother.

Afra's younger sisters, who did not understand the seriousness of their parents' fights, poked her. 'You are always his favourite!' they cried. On days the arguments were particularly bad, their mother made their least favourite food for dinner, sloppy dhaal and aloo bhaji which she served unsmiling and they ate in silence.

But her father knew he had put off Afra's marriage for as long as he could. His mother, his sister-in-laws, everyone kept asking why he had not yet found a groom for Afra. One afternoon, when Afra was 18 and unwed for eight years longer than her mother would have preferred, her father met a man in a restaurant, a friend of a friend. His name was Abbas. He had come from England and was looking for a Bangladeshi bride.

'And what do you do there?' her father asked, prepared for the usual exaggerations the Bangladeshi men from England made about their fabricated empires of restaurants and business chains. But this man was honest.

'Right now, I do not have a job. But I am planning to find one as soon as I am settled with the woman who shall be my wife,' he replied.

'He is not like others,' Afra's father thought. 'He is not pretending to be someone he is not.' That night, he invited Abbas, his mother and his sister to meet his wife and daughter in their home.

Even though she did not feel attracted to this bald man with a moustache who was twelve years older than her, Afra could not say no to her father. Besides, she trusted his choice more than she would ever trust her mother's. Her father was her friend.

'You will go to the Queen's country,' he laughed. 'You might even drive a car,' he joked, making light despite knowing he would miss her terribly.

'But what about my studies?' she asked.

'He is an educated man,' said her father. 'He will agree to let you continue, of that I'm sure.'

Within a month, Abbas and Afra were married.

But even before his show of rage in the courtyard, Afra realised Abbas was not the straightforward, honest man her father believed him to be.

She had seen him, the night of their wedding, sipping from a green glass bottle, his eyes unblinking. Abbas barely spoke to Afra. When eventually he touched her, Afra lay motionless, her eyes shut fast and tight. Her mother had told her that this was a thing that men do, but nobody had told her it would hurt so much.

For months, neighbours have been asking, 'Why is Afra still here? Why has Abbas not come for her?'

They have enjoyed answering their own questions with their own wild speculations. Afra ignored most of them, but she is tired of their blunt curiosity peering into her life to take of it what they can and spread around. Once, she sarcastically replied that her husband had taken a second wife, an English lady with pale legs wrapped in short skirts.

'What am I supposed to say?' she said stormily to her mother who scolded her like a child when the gossip made its way back to her. 'That my husband doesn't like me? That my husband doesn't want me?'

Now, though, her mother is pleased. She can tell the neighbours that her eldest daughter is leaving for England, and that once there, her wifely duties will start. She is slightly sad to see Afra go, slightly afraid of what her daughter might do when she gets there, but she has four daughters yet to marry, headache enough, and she prays the status of an eldest daughter settled overseas may bring with it better prospects for the younger ones. And so it is better that Afra goes, her mother thinks.

'And at least the girl is still married,' she tells herself, muttering Astaghfirullah, a quick utterance to Allah for redemption, when she thinks of what could have been.

After Abbas threw her things into the courtyard, Afra, who does not normally cry, wept alone for what felt like hours, heaving silently atop the double bed made especially for the newlyweds. She cried because her husband, the man her father chose for her, called her a prostitute when she had never let herself be touched before and it hurt her badly to hear the slur. She cried from anger and because she felt deceived. Mostly, she cried because she did not know what or how the rest of her life with this man would be. She had heard the gossip start, taunting and tactless, just after her wedding day; that Abbas was a drunk and that Abbas was depressed. She had heard from the servant girl that Abbas had threatened to marry an English girl, which prompted his mother to collapse and his brother to order him back to Bangladesh where he had set up a meeting with the father of an eligible bride in a restaurant.

'So that's why,' she realised. 'That's why he hates me.'

But as the call for evening prayers came, she splashed her face and clenched her jaw and vowed not to let her in-laws see her cry. She prayed and then decided she would return to her parents' house. She announced her decision to her in-laws steelily.

'If I am not wanted here, I will not stay,' she said.

Her in-laws gathered around her and promised Abbas would not always be like this. Her brother-in-law cycled quickly to fetch her parents to persuade her not to leave, for a bride simply could not walk out of her marital home so soon. But her father cried when he saw her.

'My beti, what a mistake I made choosing this man,' he said, clasping Afra's hands and breaking her heart into a million tiny shards of splintered glass that would never quite fit perfectly back into place again. 'Allah will never forgive me. I will take you back.' But before Afra could collapse into his embrace, her sister-in-law and aunts-in-law hurried him away.

'This is something for the women,' they shooed. 'Let us women sort it out.'

Her mother sat next to her on one side of her bed, her mother-in-law on the other. Each woman held one of Afra's hands. Her mother spoke first.

'I know you are determined. But you are the only one of my five daughters who is married. You are the eldest. If you leave this house, what will your sisters do? Think of them. Think of me. Think of the family's shame.'

Afra tried to speak, tried to resist, tried to tell her mother that she would look after her sisters herself, make sure they got better than this. She tried to tell her that she would be no burden, that she would work as a bank clerk and earn her own keep. But she was numb and exhausted and her body ached. The words did not come.

'If you leave this marriage, Afra,' said her mother, continuing more firmly now, 'I will have no choice but to leave this world myself. Promise me you will not leave.'

Bewildered, Afra turned her head slowly and, yet slower still, understood. She understood that her mother's pledge left her bound in this marriage to a man her father had met just once in a restaurant before deciding he was right for her. She did not begrudge her father; he was not to have known.

'All couples fight like this,' her mother-in-law said. 'Understanding comes later. I will take care of you myself. I promise you.'

And like that, her decision was made. Afra could not leave Abbas, even if he himself went away, not with her mother's threat to take her life laid out before her. Much to her surprise, her mother-in-law kept her promise and looked after her well. As soon as Abbas was gone, private tutors were arranged so she could catch up on her studies and finish her degree. Though the rest of the family, Abbas's sisters and aunts, complained it was not necessary, her mother-in-law stood firm. 'I promised her this much,' she said. Even though Afra could never quite shake the feeling that her mother-in-law was motivated into kindness more by the fear that her son might marry an English woman than by a promise to her daughter-in-law, between them a surprising friendship was formed.

But despite her mother-in-law's company, Afra has felt alone this year. She agreed to write letters to Abbas, although they are dull and formulaic, telling him what they had to eat, what she did that day. She has not told him that sometimes, she feels stunted, dead inside. He does not reply to her directly, sending his replies addressed to his mother and brother instead. The understanding her mother-in-law spoke of has not come yet.

When Abbas arrives home, there is a commotion in the courtyard as his family clusters around him.

'Where is Afra? Come, meet your husband!' her mother-in-law shouts not unkindly, up towards Afra's room. She goes downstairs. He nods salaam and Afra slightly bows her head.

'So, this is our reunion,' she thinks. 'This is how he greets me. My husband.' Later, in the middle of the night, Abbas comes to bed. He touches Afra again but they do not speak.

Afra has said goodbye to her sisters and her parents and her brother again and again over the last six weeks while Abbas has been back. She promises her sisters she will write to them and tell them all about England and the Royal Family. But it is not until they arrive at the airport that their goodbyes are final.

Afra has never left Bangladesh before and inside she feels something like electricity popping in her stomach in quick, sharp, short bursts. Her parents sob and this makes her feel heavy and sad.

'You are in Allah's hands now,' says her father. 'He will take care of you.' Her mother wails and sniffs prayers loudly over her head while her mother-in-law dabs the corner of her damp eyes with a shawl. Abbas's mother is used to airport goodbyes for she has seen Abbas off to England many times. Her cries are quieter, those of a parent accustomed to waving off an immigrant child. Afra's brother is the last to embrace her.

'England is a free country, I have heard,' he says in her ear. 'But if I hear anything about you, any scandal at all, any of this talk of leaving him again, then there will be news for you. Now go, and be good.' Afra does not cry as she waves goodbye.

Afra has not been on a plane before and Abbas snorts at her when she inhales sharply as they take off and she tightens her fists over the armrests. When she vomits into a paper bag, he shakes his head. She spends the flight vomiting and sleeping and praying and, sometimes, fighting back tears. She thinks of her father and misses him but remembers his glee, his voice declaring, 'You are going to the land of the Queen!' She thinks of what he used to say when she was a child, about her driving a car one day. She wonders if in England, that might be true and a hint of a smile tickles her face.

The cold in England is frighteningly deep. It is winter and the snow, which Afra has only seen in pictures before, is far harsher than its beauty portrays. She is shaken by it. She realises, embarrassed, her mother and mother-in-law were right to press her to take more clothes. But then how was she to know? Abbas never spoke to her of what to expect. He never speaks to her at all.

They land in London, sleeping overnight in a damp spare room belonging to a distant acquaintance Abbas knows, before catching the train northwards the next day. All the while, Afra has not been able to stop being sick. When she vomits, Abbas glances, derision curling his lip, at his overseas bride who is not built for a climate like this.

'I must not let him see me like this,' Afra thinks. 'I must not let him think I am weak.'

But it is hard for her. She cannot eat and she wonders if this is what it is like to be homesick even though she insists to herself she does not miss Sylhet one bit. Weeks later, their landlady, a kind Bangladeshi woman named Bilqis who lends Afra cardigans and charges Abbas rent at £30 a week, takes her to hospital. Bilqis, who has three young children whom Afra plays with, is right.

'You are expecting your first child,' the doctor says. 'Congratulations.'

That day, Bilqis, Afra and the children celebrate with ice creams and Lucozade, two of the few things that soften Afra's relentless morning sickness. Bilqis buys Afra a navy blue sari from an Indian fabric store for £10. 'A gift for the mother-to-be,' she says.

Abbas works at the Taj Mahal restaurant every night until midnight, and when eventually they are awake at the same time long enough to speak, Afra tells him.

'I won't look after this baby,' he tells her, monotonously. 'You will have to do it alone.' He turns over, his back a bare wall before her, and goes to sleep.

Afra does not cry, nor does she argue. She may be bound to Abbas for life by her mother's blackmail, but she resolves she will not owe him anything. Besides, she does not feel alone any more. 'My baby,' she writes in a letter to her sisters to tell them the news. 'My baby is all mine! I am so happy. No one can take my baby away from me!'

The snow thaws into spring and the sourness of her morning sickness fades and, renewed with purpose, Afra begins to think of what to do here, in England. She borrows Bilqis's sewing machine, turning fabric scraps into pretty little dresses because she is convinced her baby is a girl.

Bilqis, impressed by Afra's sewing, offers her 50p to alter this child's trousers or the other child's skirts.

'Can you sew Bangladeshi clothes?' she asks.

'I can sew anything,' Afra replies, confidently.

Slowly, young Bangladeshi and Pakistani brides from Durham and Newcastle, friends of Bilqis, come to Afra with sari blouses that need taking in or necklines and hemlines they want her to edge with rolls of colourful brocades for 50p. On Bilqis's advice, she saves the money secretly from her husband, sewing while Abbas works both afternoons and nights. Sometimes she spends the money, buying fabric for herself, making simple clothes to add to her small wardrobe or yet more tiny dresses for her baby. In the mornings, she wakes early while Abbas still sleeps, walking to the library where she spends hours reading Agatha Christie, whispering English words to her soon to be English-born baby. She barely sees Abbas, who is at the restaurant or with his friends, all the time.

With Bilqis and her small circle of new friends, the chattering women she stitches clothes for and the ladies who work at the library, Afra feels lively like a college girl again.

They take trips to Newcastle to browse large department stores. Afra spends hours in the haberdashery floors, fingering the soft fabric of beautiful dresses for baby girls which, even with her sewing money, she can scarcely afford. She vows to buy at least one for her daughter, whom she has already named Amina. 'She will be like me, but she will have more than me,' she thinks, a hand absentmindedly resting on her stomach. 'Whatever I can give to her, I shall.'

Afra plans for Amina's future. One day, she asks Bilqis for directions to Durham University and finds the office in the maths department. Proudly, she thrusts them copies of her Bangladeshi college degree and asks what she needs to do to enrol. But she is disheartened when she leaves, embarrassed she did not realise her limitations. 'We can't accept an overseas student on a visa just like that,' the clipped accented woman in the administrative office says. 'Besides, you're about to give birth anytime now.'

Amina is born during a hot, still night in the summer of 1981. Abbas takes her to the hospital but asks not to be woken when the baby comes. 'I need my sleep, I have to work,' he says.

Afra does not care because time stops still with Amina. She is all Afra can absorb, gazing at her for hours.

'Amina,' she whispers when the baby is handed to her in a moment so precious her heart feels full again. 'Amina, my child.'

Abbas receives stern letters from his family in Bangladesh. People are gossiping, saying Abbas cannot look after his baby and his wife, mocking that the three of them live in a rented room alone. Once again, the family faces shame, his brother tells him. 'You must behave as is expected of you,' his brother writes. 'Be a man.'

Abbas comes back to Bilqis's house and tells her they are moving out. He has acquired a loan of £10,000 from an acquaintance and found a flat for them in Newcastle to buy. Afra never asks whom he has borrowed the money from. She does not want to know. She does not want to go, either, but Abbas never asked her how she feels. 'I need you to pay me £50 a month for the loan,' he tells her instead. 'That is your share.'

Afra wonders what her father would say if he knew her husband demanded money of her. But what little she knows of Abbas from their short years of marriage, she is not surprised.

'Such a beautiful girl, married to such a miserable man,' Bilqis says sadly, shaking her head as Afra, holding Amina, leaves.

Newcastle is difficult for Afra. She misses Bilqis and her three children and her friends. She misses the library, where the ladies behind the counter always waved at her and never complained when she brought Amina in.

The man in the flat downstairs is a drunk. He leers at Afra, even while she carries the baby. She does not feel safe. Abbas loses his job, it is too far for him to travel to the Taj Mahal every day, and he stays home, a green bottle in his hands when he is not sleeping. Without Bilqis's sewing machine, she can make no money either. Afra hates this place. She plans to leave.

But every time she prepares, finding out train times to London and calculating how long it will take her to save for a ticket, she is held back. She remembers her mother, who would rather take her own life than see her child divorced. She remembers her brother, and his unforgiving farewell at the airport suggesting she would be disowned if she dared leave her marriage. And so, every time she wishes she could take Amina and leave Abbas, she stops.

Then, she remembers the notebook her father gave to her two years ago before she left Bangladesh, filled with addresses and phone numbers of friends of her father settled in London, people she calls uncles and aunts but are not blood relatives. 'They will help you,' he had said. Afra is wary; she knows all too well how anything she might say, the slightest hint of a complaint about her life, might work its way back to her family, a few elaborations added along the way.

But she also knows she is alone here. She has seen for herself, through Bilqis and her friends, how those who have left their homeland have come together to form a chain that strengthens each of them, a web spun tightly spreading out wide. They call each other baji. They are each other's family, displaced and far away. Alone in Newcastle, Afra does not have this and she realises it is what she needs. She cannot count on Abbas. She must do something.

While Abbas sleeps, Afra takes Amina to a payphone, counting out coins carefully. She calls the first number.

'But why did you not call earlier? I was expecting to hear from you when your father first wrote to me,' says the uncle, a man she vaguely remembers from her childhood, on the other end of the line. She explains, carefully and shyly, that her husband has lost his job. 'Well you must come here to London! I have a friend who runs a travel agency. He needs people to work for him. Bring your husband, he is an educated man, no?'

There is only one way to convince Abbas to board the train to London. Afra has used up most of her money, saved from sewing, to buy the tickets. She tells him she will go to London with Amina without him and, then, what would his brother and mother say? First he refuses and raises his voice, but even Abbas can see that a free ticket to London and the promise of a job is reason enough to leave, better than hearing from his family how he has failed, again and again.

In Tower Hamlets, Afra's uncle and his wife welcome them into their flat on top of a restaurant in a noisy street where Afra notices Bangladeshi men huddled together, chewing betal leaves. Abbas is polite and it surprises Afra, for she has never seen him like this. She wonders if this is how he charmed her father five years ago.

'When I last saw you, you were just a child!' her uncle says to her. 'And now – look!' Amina shyly clutches Afra's leg, until her uncle prises her away with chocolate. The gesture almost makes Afra cry, tears suddenly at the brink of spilling onto her cheeks as she realises, overwhelmed, just how lonely she has been. Bilqis was a friend, a good one at that, but she has missed the presence of elders of her father's generation who always seem to know what to do.

Abbas is taken to the travel agency and meanwhile, her aunt shows her an empty flat on a nearby council estate that a friend of theirs has said Abbas and Afra can live in for a while. It is small and empty, run down with just a mattress, and there is rubbish piled high in the corner which Afra tells Amina not to touch. For now, it will do. While her aunt apologises for the state it is in and for not having enough room in their own home, which is already full, Afra shakes her head. 'No, no,' she says. 'This is more than enough.'

As they walk back, they are stopped by women in saris who greet her aunt cordially. Some of them live in the same estate, her aunt explains.

'This is Afra, she is coming from Newcastle. She is Imtiaz's daughter, from Sylhet,' she says.

The women nod, as if they know her father by name. They smile at her, knowing what it is like to be a stranger in a city like this. There are offers of chai and pots and pans she can borrow to cook. 'We have not moved our things yet,' she says shyly. 'Does anyone have a sewing machine?'

Afra begins to sew furiously in their bare flat on a machine borrowed from a neighbour, working her way through bags of skirts and trousers made to sell in high street stores that a man brings from the factories, knocking on all the women's doors, and then later comes to collect. She earns £1 a piece while Abbas is in the travel agency; it is more than she ever made before.

But it is not enough. Afra is losing weight, feeding only Amina and Abbas whenever he comes home late at night, and her health suffers. A health visitor, Beverley, comes during the day. 'Amina is happy but you cannot live like this,' she says. 'You are ill. But you are also educated and you speak good English and you can do so much more than this.'

Beverley checks up on Afra every few weeks and as her strength returns, she gives her an application form. 'We need women like you,' Beverley says. 'We need interpreters to help us speak to Bangladeshi women, to understand what they need. Promise me you'll fill it out.'

All Afra has ever wanted is the chance to stand on her own two feet. Finally, it is there before her in an application form and a brief interview, and it is there eventually in a hospital staff identity card stamped with her name. She is paid every month, a small but substantial salary, and most of it is hers.

She tells Abbas she has a job as a hospital cleaner and that her pay is less than it is. They are white lies, and she prays to Allah to forgive her for them, but as she picks Amina up from her school gates every day, she knows they are necessary.

Abbas acknowledges her in small ways more now, picking up groceries occasionally, asking her what things they need. He does not forbid her to work and this suits Afra, to not know her husband or care where he has been or have to tell him everything.

After years apart, Afra's parents come to England. Abbas sullenly agreed to help find cheap tickets through the travel agency which Afra saved for years to contribute towards. Afra is overjoyed. It has been too long. At the airport, she breathes them in, smelling her home and her sisters and her childhood in their clothes and on their skin.

She takes them to Abbas's secondhand car and watches her father's face as she takes the driver's seat. Beverley, who has become a good friend, had told her learning to drive was necessary and had helped arrange lessons on weekends, taking care of Amina while Afra struggled with three-point turns. Beverley and Amina baked a celebratory cake when she came home, laughing, waving a licence in her hands.

'I will take you to our home,' Afra says to her parents. Her father giggles like a child, amazed and playful.

'I told you,' he says to her mother when eventually he recovers enough from his wonderment to speak. 'I told you! I always said, that one day this girl, she would drive a car and take me around. And here we are!'

The month they spend together is the last time Afra sees her parents. Her father beams with pride each day as she leaves for work, and both he and her mother dote on Amina, their first grandchild, whose infancy they only witnessed through rare photos sent preciously through the post.

But years later, phone calls come, one by one, in the night. Frantic ones, bad news, devastating news crackling down a breaking phone-line punctuated by heart-wrenching cries.

Afra mourns quietly and alone. She does not want Amina to see. She misses her parents desperately and now that she is older, she understands. She understands that they only tried to give her something better and something more through marriage and while that may not have been Abbas, it has always been there in Amina, her joy, and in London and her job.

Afra made a promise to her mother once, sitting on her bed as a newlywed that she would not leave her marriage or shame her family. But her mother's life is taken now and with her passing, after the grief, comes the realisation that Afra is free.

She tells Abbas, calmly after thirty years, that she is leaving him, that she has no reason to stay any more and that he can live with his mistress, with whom he has been all this time, if he agrees to a divorce.

Afra is strengthened by Amina, a clever young woman now, and it is Amina who helps them find their own home to buy, filled with books and plants and Miss Marple films that sometimes the two of them watch together on Sundays, while the rain falls in teardrops outside.

2

In the cracks

I would be lying if I told you I thought about you all the time.

It isn't because I don't miss you. I do. But I just don't miss you all the time.

It doesn't work that way. It doesn't work that way when you left me so long ago. It doesn't work that way when I haven't even had the chance to grieve for you for twenty-two years.

I'm sorry, love, but you left me no choice. It all happened so fast. There was so much to do as soon as you'd gone. But I've finally got time now.

Vijay left today, packed up all of his things. I suppose that's it. He's the last one, leaving the nest as they say. For the first time in twenty-two years, it's just me.

I'm sat here on my own on the sofa with a cup of strong tea and I can hear the clock ticking in the front room, it's that quiet.

I've waited for this moment for a long time, I've known it was coming and I've dreaded it, but I think it will do me some good to breathe out.

Now that the house is still and now that I am finally alone, I'll just sit here and take stock awhile. If you don't mind, I'll begin right now.

You left me with the whole lot, you know: the children to look after, the house to sort out, not least both of our families to deal with too. I bet you didn't think about all that, did you?

So I had no time for grief and certainly no time for the rituals of our religion. No, I didn't wear a white sari. And no, of course I didn't shave my head. Besides, you always liked me with long hair. Oh, stop. We shouldn't joke about our traditions. It's very disrespectful, might I add.

Anyhow, as if any Hindu wives up north do those things. Oh, all right, maybe the saris, but certainly not the hair. Thank God we're not in some village back in India. Can you imagine?

I didn't think you'd mind too much, that I didn't do those wifely, widow things. If anything you'd probably have told me to go straight to the pub. 'Talk to Rosa and Lily, next time they come in,' you'd have said. 'They'll make you feel better. Chin up, love!'

As it happens, I still see Rosa and Lily and some of the other English ladies we used to serve. A few of them even came to Nahul's wedding. I wasn't too keen on us being pub landlords in the beginning, but I'll tell you what, it gave me some lifelong friends in the end who have been with me longer than you ever were. I can't begrudge any of that.

Your old pub friends couldn't believe it when they heard you'd gone. They left bunches of roses at the front door, that I suppose the wives had bought, with notes written in biro turned watery from the rain, offering their sympathy, the things people always say. They called you Sat, because they never could say your full name, and told you to RIP. That sort of thing. Most of them wrote kind, exuberant things about you, calling you their favourite landlord, saying they'd always raise a glass in remembrance of you. I'm sure you'd have liked that.

Nahul and Vijay pop in to The Albion from time to time. Some of your regulars are still there. They buy the boys a drink, refer to them as Sat's lads. I suppose it's nice for them, a little reminder of you. There's so much talk about immigrants now that the boys can't quite believe there was a time that Indian pub landlords even existed. I'm not sure I could imagine doing it now.

I suppose our pub days were quite unusual. I think the children like that we did it. I think it makes them feel like we stood out from the other Asian families around here. They quite like to tell people that they spent a small part of their childhood living above a pub. They find it quite funny, to be honest, that their old mum even served behind the bar on occasion, even though you know I wasn't as keen on doing that as you were.

The first time I met Nahul's university friends at his graduation, they were so surprised to hear my voice, my Bolton accent thick and strong as it ever was. I think they expected me to sound like I had come from India, speaking English with a heavy accent like so many of the others do. Some of them even talked to me slowly as if I couldn't understand otherwise.

Ha! I've been here since I was 14, I told them. And then you should have seen the look on some of their faces! I teased Nahul for a long time after that, about his posh English friends. He did admit he found their reaction to me quite amusing too.

I kept them for a long time, all the sympathy notes and the cards, in a large tin at the bottom of the bookshelf in the lounge. But then, you know, I had to start making room once Lisha and Ellora came along because their toys get everywhere, and I realised I didn't want to keep that tin any more.

Don't take this the wrong way, love, but I don't think I will ever want to read them again. I haven't even looked at them since I first put them away. So I got rid of that tin and everything in it. I just threw them out. Yes, in the bin.

Oh love, they were just cards. They weren't you. I needed to move on, and having them sat there at the bottom of the bookshelf in the lounge, well, it didn't help. That's all.

What's that you say? You don't recognise this place? Well, no you wouldn't. We've changed things quite a lot over the years.

The last time we redecorated was last year. Vijay and Nahul paid for it all and said I could get whatever I liked. I've got a sparkling new bathroom and the kitchen of my dreams, with glossy cabinets and a coffee machine. They are so generous, my boys. Our boys, yes.

But it isn't as if there's no trace of you whatsoever, love. There's a photo of you in the entrance hall, right by the door, and I always keep small strings of flowers around the frame. It's one of the rituals I do like to keep. I didn't wallpaper over your memory, didn't throw you out along with the sympathy cards, if that's what you're thinking. You're still here, in the cracks between the bricks.

I never was too happy about raising the children in the flat above the pub so I'm glad you gave it up before you left. It would have been an even bigger nightmare for me to sort out the lease on that place. But you didn't make it easy for me, you know, leaving me to buy our council house and then pay a mortgage on it all on my own and that too on a teaching-assistant salary.

Sometimes I wonder how I did it. Three children under 10, and no husband to help with any of it. My friends say it's a big achievement. They say I should be proud. But I don't see it like that.

I know no better. It was just something I got on with.

I was never keen on living in a council house in the first place; it wasn't something my dad ever agreed with. He always said, 'One should own one's house,' so I made sure that I did, in the end. I just had to get on with it, finish what you'd started.

I suppose it's in my blood, getting on with things. Mum and dad, they were workers. Grafters. They worked longer hours than anyone would ever believe up in that textile mill. It's how they raised all of us.

'Roll up your sleeves and get on with it,' that's what they always said. And I'm glad of it, believe me, I am. I couldn't have just been one of those widows who sat there and let her family and her in-laws take command, dependent on others for pocket money like a child. No. I couldn't have been one of those widows. I had to keep going, for the sake of the children, for the sake of my own life.

But Saatvik, I've been grafting for twenty-two years now, rolling up my sleeves and getting on with it. On my own. And sometimes I feel so angry with you. I'm wiped out, exhausted, just hearing your voice in my head.

I'm so tired sometimes. I wish I could just curl up on this sofa right now, and shut my eyes.

You never told me it was lung cancer. I suppose you didn't want to upset me, after seeing how devastated I was when Mum died.

Oh, my love. If only you'd said.

I hated your cigarettes. I still do. But if you'd said something, if you'd told me, well, we could have gone to the hospital together. We could have done something. I could've helped you give your habit up. And not just me, your brothers too. We all could've helped. We could have at least tried.

But, no, you kept it to yourself and you even took that chance of us helping you away.

I don't mean to sound angry. I know you were right to have done what you did, kept it to yourself. Even if you'd have told me, it'd have made no difference. It was too late.

They told me afterwards at the hospital that it was chronic. They couldn't believe I didn't know.

I felt cheated then, because you kept it to yourself and the cancer that killed you was self-inflicted. But I suppose, in a strange way, that made it easier to accept. Because you did it to yourself. All those cigarettes. It's not as if you stepped into the middle of a busy road, not looking where you were going. It's not as if it was sheer bad luck.

Looking around this room, this house, I'm glad I redecorated so many times. Because if I close my eyes, I can go back in time and see all of our old things and see you, standing in the kitchen doorway holding the plastic box of sandwiches I'd made for your lunch. I can see you, the sweat dripping off your forehead and dampening your shirt all of a sudden. I can hear you too, saying you don't feel right, and then I can see you again, shaking your head, falling to the floor. I can see myself, twenty-two years younger, screaming and shaking as I pick up the telephone. I can see the paramedics rushing in. I can see them, trying to do their best. But then I can feel the kind one, the female one, putting her arms around me while I can hear the other one, declaring the time of death.

I'm glad I've changed things because I don't think I could bear it if that was all I could see in here, every single day.

Raashi turns 30 this year. Thirty, I know. She's not that much younger than I was when you died.

She's doing so well. She works at one of the biggest law firms in the country. She's got aspirations, things I never had. The idea of university or having a proper career, well, that was out of the question for me. She asks me about it sometimes: 'Mum, did you ever want to be more than a teaching assistant?' I don't have an answer for her. I don't know what I could have been. When she was a teenager, she used to cut out jobs advertised in the local newspaper and leave them on the fridge for me. Translator jobs in the law courts. Administrative jobs at banks. Once she got excited about a vacancy she'd seen in *The Times*, the proper paper, for Asian interpreters required by the security service. I laughed so much. Raashi honestly thought I should have applied.

Aspirations! I never had any. My job was enough for me. And I loved it. I went back to work five weeks after you left. The headteacher, Mrs Sheldon, came round soon after you'd passed away and told me to take all the time that I needed.

But I knew I had to get back.

I've already told you, I couldn't have been one of those widows whose own life stopped still just because her husband's had. I needed to keep working and keep on earning.

Besides, the children in the classroom brought me such joy. They helped me more than they will ever know. Perhaps I could have been a teacher, if I'd had a chance to do the training. But I don't regret it; no. I did what I needed to do to take care of my children and that's the most important thing.

Maybe that's what I'll tell Raashi, when she asks me again.

Married? Oh, Raashi would roll her eyes at you for asking that. I have to say, I do fret about her sometimes. Of course I'd like her to meet a young man, but she says she's in no rush. I wish she'd find someone. I've tried introducing her to boys, boys that other people have told me about, but things are so different from our time. Times have changed and that makes me feel old.

Raashi, she knows what she wants. I wonder sometimes if there is someone she hasn't told me about. She doesn't say. I'd like him to be an Indian boy, but I suppose I can accept it if it doesn't happen that way. That's the difference between this new generation and ours. We accepted our parents' decision and let them have the final say, and now it's the other way round.

Do you remember? 'Married by 20, all of you!' That's what my dad said. And we were, as well. Perhaps I should ask one of her brothers to organise a cricket match and invite some nice Indian lads round. See if history will repeat itself.

Don't be daft. Of course I remember. You, in your cricket whites, standing head and shoulders above the rest, me with that ridiculous beehive. You were quite cheeky for asking if you could telephone me straight away. But still, it's my favourite memory of you, my favourite memory of us. It's the one memory I've thought of, for a split second here and there, whenever I've allowed myself to.

Nahul married quite young, or at least young for his generation. He met Taani on his pharmacy degree and they were both still students when he told me he wanted to marry her. He was ever so nervous to tell me about her, but I was delighted for both of them. The wedding took place the same summer they graduated.

Sat, that was a beautiful summer. I don't miss you every day, but there have been several occasions when I've thought to myself that I shouldn't have to be alone. It took me a long time to get used to being at gatherings with our Indian friends where everyone was part of a couple. I was so happy but I felt so alone on Nahul's wedding day.

I wish you had been there too.

Taani is a lovely daughter-in-law. She takes such good care of me. And she makes such an effort with the girls, to make sure they stay in touch with their roots. Would you believe, Ellora's only 3 and she's already saying Gujarati words as easily as she speaks English. Taani takes Lisha to khattak dance classes and both of the little ones love dressing up in Indian suits. They do so make my heart full, my granddaughters. Your granddaughters, too. Lisha points at your photograph sometimes, and asks what you might be up to and I make something up.

It is really quite touching, seeing Nahul becoming a dad. In some ways, he reminds me of you.

As for Vijay, well he's still so young. I call him my baby sometimes and he pulls away and says, 'Mum, don't!'

I can't believe he moved out today. If I let myself, I might stop and weep. He said he'd phone me every day and I nearly burst into tears there and then, as soon he'd said it. Such a sweet boy, and a handsome one too. The company he is going to work for is only small, but I have no doubt that he'll do well for himself and soon work his way up the ladder.

All three of my children, our children, they know the meaning of hard work and I'm so proud of them for that.

Does Vijay remember you? I … I'm sorry, love. I know this must be hard to hear. But he was only 3 when you left us, and I suppose he must not have any memories of you. He knows bits of you, like pieces of a jigsaw puzzle, things he has heard about you from other people here and there. He knows your love of cricket, parties, the way you used to style your hair. But he doesn't actually remember anything. How could he, though? He was so young.

Raashi remembers slightly more, I think, but, now don't get upset, love, it's not something we talk about much. Let me say this as gently as I can: I'm not sure Raashi and Vijay can relate to you much, beyond the photograph of you on the wall.

You can't blame them for not knowing who you were. I suppose they're more used to life without a dad in it than with.

Now, this will cheer you up. Nahul remembers you. Yes, I'm sure. He asks me every now and then if I remember when you did this or that.

He remembers things like that holiday we took to the Lake District in the borrowed caravan. He remembers the pub better than the other two can.

There were times I used to wonder how it would affect the three of them, not having a dad around. There were times it was so very difficult, Sat. Teenagers aren't easy, those were the hardest years. All I wanted was for them to succeed and do well at school, and I think they all went through phases of resenting me for that.

Everything has worked out now, but it is harder than you might think, trying to be both a mum and a dad.

I tried to do as much as I could for them, growing up. Holidays, school trips, even football matches. But still. I don't know if I did half of it the way you would have. We never really planned that far ahead, did we?

Since you left us, my whole life has been about the children. And now that they have grown up, they do so much for me in return. I have everything I need. I don't ask them for anything and because I've been careful with money all my life, I have plenty of savings for my small wants.

But the children are always spoiling me.

When I take the train down to see Raashi in London, she plans all sorts of things for us to do. We see theatre shows, visit museums, try out new restaurants. Nahul's arranging a family holiday for us to all go to Tunisia next year. Vijay always told me to put my feet up on the weekend and he'd take care of everything. I'll miss his Sunday roasts, but it won't be long before he's back up to visit on the weekend anyway. It's a warm feeling, to be looked after. I don't feel alone when I think of my children. Our children.

I always used to see the sons and daughters of the Indian doctors, walking to and from school in their tidy uniforms for their private school, and I wanted to give our children that chance. But I knew there was no way I could afford an expensive education, so I did what I could with them at home instead. Oh, they hated it, sitting inside around the kitchen table in the holidays doing past papers and verbal reasoning tests while all the other children in the street played outside.

But it paid off. I'm ever so proud of who they've become.

Don't feel sad, Sat. I know you've missed out on knowing them, but our children have turned out all right. They're decent adults. They're responsible. They're determined. They've done well for themselves.

It's the sort of thing you see in the papers, stories about the hard-working children of immigrants. Well, it's true. We're grafters, all of us

I have just one regret. My children, our children, they're not religious. I've tried, but I don't know what they believe or if they believe at all.

But, Sat, I still pray. Oh, but the prayers I whisper for you are endless in my heart. There have been so many times I felt tested and cheated by your death, but our scriptures taught me patience and strength and acceptance. Our faith calmed me down.

But my children, our children, they've never been interested in any of that. Religion aside, I'm not sure they even feel that Indian either.

Perhaps it's my fault. Maybe I wasn't as strict with them as our parents were with us. Dad never even let us cut out hair short or wear skirts at home. But I don't think I'd have got anywhere trying to tell Raashi what she could and couldn't wear. I've only taken the children once to India and they were downright miserable. They stuck out like anything, my little Westerners, poor things. They spent the whole time counting down the days until they could come home again.

At least Taani is not like that. At least she can make up for my mistakes and pass some of our culture along to the girls.

But please Sat, don't blame me. I had to do it all on my own. There was only so much I could pass on to them. There is only so much they could inherit in their blood from us; their names, the colour of their skin. The rest of them is as English as can be. I suppose it's only natural. I mean, after all, their dad did run a pub.

I've allowed myself to cry today.

It's been four hours since Vijay left and as soon as he shut the door, I sobbed my heart out.

He phoned me a few hours ago, to say that he'd reached Birmingham safe and sound and he's picked up the keys to the flat he's renting.

I told him I'm fine. And I am, really, I am. I feel much better now.

I don't often cry. In fact, I've only cried a few times since you left. Oh, I've been on the brink of tears more times than I can count but I've always somehow managed to hold back. I've got a knack for that. I think it must come from my dad. He was no-nonsense like that. But I let myself cry today and, do you know what, it's been twenty-two years and I've not grieved for you properly, so I think that's all right.

I remember one of the times I did cry, really did cry, was soon after you died.

It was when all the relatives had finally gone. I sensed the pity of them all, creeping over me. I'd seen the look in their eyes, the fear they felt for me. And then they left too. That's when the sadness came to me.

The children had already gone back to school by then, because I didn't think it was right for them to be off for so long, so I'd long since sent them up to bed. I sat on our old sofa and ate a sandwich from a plate on my lap because I was sick of the taste of curries everyone had made for us and left in the fridge. Then, I put my head in my hands and pushed my face into a cushion so the children wouldn't hear. And I sobbed with the weight of all of my body, the way you sob when your heart's been broken. I pitied myself, the way others pitied me. I don't know if you've ever cried like that because I doubt you'd ever needed to. Or maybe you did, when they told you it was cancer, and you just never said.

I sobbed for a good hour, and afterwards I drank three glasses of water in a row because I felt like I'd shrivelled up inside, like all those tears had left me dry.

I switched on the telly then, in time for the news, and there was this poor young Kurdish woman who had fled from her home in Iraq. She had five of her own children and a handful of nephews and nieces to look after. They had nothing to eat, so this poor woman, she walked up and down the mountains collecting snow with her hands and melting it in a pot to make water for the children to drink.

I sat there, and I watched this woman walking up and down the mountain, and I thought, 'My life is nothing like hers.' I had a roof over my head, I had food to feed my children. You were gone. But my world had not ended. And that's what it took for me. That poor woman's lot is what it took for me to get up off that sofa and stop feeling sorry for myself.

I went to bed and the next day I decided to go back to work. I made a choice. I make that choice every day.

I suppose that's perspective, isn't it? It's what has kept me going all these twenty-two years. It was only after that night that I realised what I needed to do. It was only after that night that I realised where my place was. That it wasn't to move to India like some of our relatives suggested, that it wasn't to remarry and share the responsibility of raising my children with someone else. No. That wasn't what I needed to do at all.

The day you left me could have been the day that I gave up. Though we were not married for long, we had made a start on something, you and I. And I made a choice to carry it on alone. I made a choice to keep on living.

I don't miss you every day, my love, but that doesn't mean I've forgotten you. I think of you every now and then in split seconds, flashbacks from our life.

It's the only way, after so long. I can't imagine who you'd be now, if you'd lived twenty-two years longer, but I hope you'd still be the man I married. Perhaps you'd be less of a risk-taker with age. Perhaps you'd look after your health more. But I don't let myself think about those sort of things for too long. I can't change the past. I can't change who I've become. I can't change the things that we've been through and I can't take back that day that you fell down on the floor. So I'll stop this, now. And now that I've let this all out, now that I've had this chance to take stock, I think I'll be all right.

3

The curfew

As a girl, Sara's hair hung down to her waist. Long and thick, black as the night and shiny like a pool of ink, she was complimented on it even by people she did not know.

Her mother's friends, women who all looked the same to Sara in their floral-printed shalwar kameez, stroked her head, picking up silky strands then letting them fall through their fingers again. 'Mashallah, mashallah,' they said. 'This one, one day she'll make a beautiful bride!'

Sara had green eyes like her grandfather. Her mother's friends tipped her chin backwards, peering into shimmering irises flashing the colour of rare peacock feathers. 'Mashallah, mashallah,' they said, approving of Sara's marketable, marriageable attributes apparent at such a young age. 'Such pretty eyes!' they murmured to her mother, one or two enquiring once more after Sara's age.

But Sara did not feel pretty. At 12 years old, unusually tall for her age, she was uncomfortable with the attention her hair and her eyes and her body, painfully adjusting under the spotlight of puberty, had already acquired.

In Pakistan, on a family visit to Jhelum to see her father's relatives, faces who looked familiar but whose names she did not always know, she felt watched by labourers toiling in the dry, hot streets. She felt eyes fall upon her, scan her slowly up and down. She knew her mother's friends did not, at least, look at her like this. She felt ashamed.

Sara told her mother, but her mother shrugged her shoulders. 'This is the burden of beauty,' she said. 'Or you could cover up instead.'

Her mother took her to the tailor, a sweaty booth in the covered market where a fluorescent tube light fizzed from the heat and Sara stood, arms out and awkward, while a man circled her chest with tape, measuring her between her shoulder blades and around her waist. Her mother searched through multicoloured fabrics, piled high in heaps from floor to ceiling, tugging this way and that through mounds of material for the most opaque she could find.

Sara's new shalwar kameez were plainer and looser than the ones she wore before and far too thick to wear under the unforgiving sun. But still, she felt men watching her, as she walked swiftly down the street and disappeared through the mud-flecked gates of her father's family house.

Sara's father had hitchhiked to England from Jhelum long before she was born. She did not understand why they had to come back here.

Sara's mother was proud. She stacked up the compliments her youngest daughter received, storing them as evidence of some measure of maternal success. After all, Sara was her daughter; her beauty came from genes.

'People will notice you,' she counselled Sara, while brushing her long, thick hair. 'You are older now. Soon your time will come. These are the things men and their mothers look for in marriage; a pretty, good, quiet girl.'

Later, back home in west London, Sara stood in the bathroom staring at the mirror, her flashing green eyes and her dark long hair taunting her. In one hand, she held her mother's sewing scissors. Trembling, she clutched a fistful of hair and made the first cut. She could not do it smoothly and it did not fall in one, clean line. But the scissors were sharp and quickly, bit by bit, she snipped coarsely until it hung, jagged and wild, at the top of her shoulders.

'She is going to kill you,' her older sister, Mariam, said.

Sara's mother did not talk to her for days. Then, she pulled out a few crumpled notes from her purse and shoved them in Sara's hand, ordering her to a hairdresser to sort her self-inflicted mess out. Sara had been scared but she smiled to herself now. In some small way, she was winning.

Life at home in Hillingdon in their semi-detached house was made up of the same, never-changing routine. After their homework was done, Sara and Mariam, who was two years older, helped their mother with dinner, warming naan or boiling rice and laying the table for their two older brothers who were often never home, their absence unexplained.

Sara always set one plate aside for their father, a quiet but firm man who worked late shifts at a factory nearby and came home long after she had gone to bed. Sometimes, Sara heard him unlock the front door and step out of his shoes, her parents murmuring perfunctorily to each other before he ate his reheated meal.

On weekends while their father caught up on sleep and their brothers kept busy with part-time jobs or unquestioned social lives, Sara and Mariam accompanied their mother to the supermarket or the mosque or to the house of a family friend.

In the mosque, they listened to monotonous lectures which Sara struggled to follow. Legs curled tightly underneath her, head covered by a warm shawl, Sara slipped away into daydreams, oblivious to Mariam poking her in her side.

At the end of the lectures, their mother pushed the girls forward to say salaam to women they'd never before met. 'These are my daughters,' she would announce, while the girls would quietly answer the usual questions of how old they were and what they liked to do, before their mother took over again.

Occasionally, girls from her secondary school asked Sara to join them on Saturdays, to go shopping in Uxbridge or catch an afternoon showing of some popular film at the cinema. But her mother refused to let her go, reminding her that Pakistani teenage girls did not go out like English ones.

'You know what girls like that get up to,' she said disapprovingly.

Besides, Sara knew the rules; neither she nor Mariam were allowed into town without one of their older brothers or a parent by their side. So Sara said no to her friends the first time they asked and then the second time too and then, eventually, they stopped asking at all. As a result, Sara didn't have many friends at school. She learnt to keep herself company.

Books became her escape. She spent lunch hours in the library, discovering the Brontë sisters one by one, devouring Jane Austen and Elizabeth Gaskell.

Her English teacher, pleased at her interest, enthusiastically passed her extra reading lists, suggesting this author or that. At home, Sara closed the door to the bedroom she shared with Mariam and lost herself in novels of old-fashioned romance and heroines finding their own way.

'Always so quick to pick up a book,' quipped her mother, who had no time for fiction, except for the Bollywood kind. 'But never so quick to pick up a prayer mat, young lady.'

By now, Sara's English teacher saw potential in her and suggested university courses to which she encouraged her to apply. Sara was determined. The prospect of university, of studying a subject she loved, was the one thing that could belong to her alone, that would not require a constant chaperone.

But her parents had conditions, which she already knew because Mariam lived by the same stipulations too. Sara's choices were limited to selecting a university close enough to be back home every weekday by eight o'clock in the evening.

Her parents weren't impressed by her choice to read English, but it would do. She overheard her father placating her mother, late one night after his shift. He said, 'She will be married after university, so what does it matter what she studies now? Let her enjoy those books she loves.'

Sara accepted her parents' conditions; it was the best she could do. She chose Brunel, a university just twenty minutes away. She kept her head down and revised.

Afterwards, the wait for A-level exam results felt endlessly long. She felt listless all summer, selectively switching off from her mother's various shrieks to lay the table or do the laundry or the washing up.

She read and reread her favourite books: *Jane Eyre*, *Pride and Prejudice*, *Wuthering Heights*. Through the pages of her books, she felt part of another world in which there was romance and passion and purpose and feeling, all the things she longed for but did not yet know where to find. 'There must be more than this,' she said to herself, pulling herself off her bed to finish off chores. 'There must be more than just this.'

On her first day of university, Sara felt different. Threads of trepidation and excitement wove through her veins. It was the first time in her life she felt trusted and completely on her own. There was no Mariam to walk next to her, no older brother to navigate her through crowds.

But despite the thrill of her new sense of freedom, she was overwhelmed. Lost, she missed Mariam terribly.

For a moment, Sara contemplated taking the Tube across the city to seek out her older sister, a history student at Westminster, but more than once she hesitated and turned away at the Tube station's steps.

'You'll be fine,' Mariam assured her over the phone, calming her younger sister down. 'I'll see you at home tonight.'

'But I'm not good at meeting new people like you,' said Sara. 'I don't know what to do.'

In her English literature lectures, Sara sat near the back on her own. But the back rows were dominated by slackers, slouching and texting or listening to music or playing on their mobile phones and it made Sara, always a hard-working student, uneasy. So she inched forward, row by row, until she stopped in the middle and sat next to a girl in a checked shirt with a friendly smile and a tidy ponytail.

Annie and Sara soon became friends, swapping phone numbers and lecture notes, saving seats and sharing books.

One boy always sat in the same seat in the front row. He wore round, black glasses, had messy brown hair and looked far younger than everyone else at 18. His hand shot up to answer every question; he took notes not on a pad like everybody else but on a slim laptop instead.

'He is such a nerd!' exclaimed Annie after a particular lecture on *Vanity Fair*, and Sara laughed and agreed. They called him 'the boy with all the answers'. From then on, every time he put his hand up, Annie and Sara exchanged funny looks and rolled their eyes.

But Sara listened to his answers. She listened and she noticed him. She saw him sometimes, in the library or in the campus cafe. Once or twice she caught his eye, held it quickly before looking away, but she was not sure he recognised her.

She didn't tell Annie, but there was something about him, this boy with all the answers, that made her want to know his name.

One day, he was late and someone else had taken his place. Sara was absorbed in scribbling notes in shorthand on themes in *Bleak House* when she felt someone slip into the spare seat next to her. It was him. She fixed her eyes down at her notes. But she was distracted by his hands so close to hers, by his forearm resting casually on the writing shelf.

'Did I miss much?' he asked at the end, as they packed up their bags. 'I don't suppose I could borrow your notes?'

His name was James. After that day, the three of them began to sit together, Annie, Sara and James, in that order. Annie doodled teasing, tiny hearts in the margin of Sara's notepad during lectures, small enough so James could not see but still much to Sara's dismay. Then she started excusing herself quickly and cleverly after lectures, leaving Sara alone with James, texting her later to see how things went.

They started with coffees, walking with hot paper cups in their hands. They compared timetables, James suggesting lunch on the afternoons they both had free. This became their weekly routine. Sometimes, after study sessions they grabbed pizza or plates of pasta in the evening from one of the campus canteens, Sara inventing excuses to leave early so she could be home by eight.

Sara, who had never had so much as a schoolgirl crush, who had never properly spoken to a boy throughout her teens, felt something warm and indefinable rising inside her like a soft blush sunset.

It was simple. Within weeks, she knew. She liked James. She liked the way he talked to her, the way he listened to what she had to say. She liked his eyes and his hands and his hair. She thought he liked her too, but in a way, it almost didn't matter. What mattered was she had this, this something warm and indefinable, to escape to every day from the monotony of the home life she always had to return to.

One evening, when she was home before curfew, her mother called her into the lounge.

'I have something to show you beti, sit,' she said, patting the space next to her on the sofa. From inside a plastic wallet, her mother pulled out a glossy A6-sized photo of a Pakistani man, with a trimmed beard and slicked-back hair in a formal white jacket. 'Look. This proposal has come for you. He is 28. He runs his own business in Slough. Look!' her mother said, thrusting the photo into her lap.

'Are you serious?' Sara asked quietly.

'Serious, yes, yes,' said her mother. 'We are looking for Mariam too, but I thought this one for you. He likes to read too, just like you do.'

Sara's eyes flashed, but she knew better than to raise her voice. She may have been just shy of 20 years old, but her Pakistani mother still commanded Sara, and the rest of her children, when absolutely necessary with sharp, stinging slaps that left pink marks on their pale skin.

Sara's mother had been busy, filling out matrimonial matchmaking forms on behalf of her daughters at the mosque.

She showed Sara the copy she'd completed for her, where she'd listed her daughter's interests as reading, cooking and Bollywood. Sara noticed her own picture attached, an uncomfortable, serious portrait of her wearing a silk blue shalwar kameez from last Eid. Her mother had made her perch on this same sofa for it, alone, while one of her brothers zoomed in with the camera, trying not very hard to make her smile.

Sara hated having her picture taken because she knew what it meant, that a print would be passed around or a copy emailed from one prospective mother-in-law to another; her skin, her hair, her eyes assessed.

This time, her photograph was stapled to the matrimonial form which had been matched with potential suitors by the mosque's marriage committee, a cluster of Pakistani mothers. A woman looking for a Pakistani bride for her son, the man in the photo, had made contact.

'What do you think?' asked her mother.

'I'm not sure I'm ready,' said Sara. 'I'm still in my first year and, well, I'm not sure I'm ready.' It was the closest she could come to saying, simply, no.

Her mother's tone switched from sweet and plying to loud and sarcastic and sharp in one go, a furious condemnation in Urdu already prepared. 'I don't know what to do with you. At least Mariam considers. You, you just say no. I don't know what to do with you. You think you're some princess with your cursed green eyes? You sit there doing nothing, reading your stupid books! Go on, get out!'

Sara picked up her bag and ran straight up the narrow stairs to her room, not looking at Mariam who was already there. Dumping her bag on her bed, she crossed the hall and locked herself in the bathroom, cooling her clammy forehead against the shiny flat tiles.

She was convinced her mother somehow knew all about her secret, her longing for James, convinced she knew all about their lunches and dinners and coffees together too. Even though she still didn't know if he was attracted to her too, or couldn't quite let herself believe that he did, she knew she had to stop, before it got too much.

She began avoiding James on campus, leaving quickly after lectures and making excuses to skip pre-planned lunches. Once, she accidentally let it slip that she lived just a short distance away. He asked if he could come over one day for lunch. She panicked wildly, cried 'No! Never!' and left. He could not understand why she got so upset.

It was too much, her yearning for James. Each time she let herself consider the possibility of even so much as holding his hand, she felt it was a sin. She felt a knot curl hard in her ribs and in her chest and she knew it was a bad sign if she thought of him, and felt pain.

At night she could not sleep, stumbling over obstacles in her mind, wondering what to tell him, how to make him understand that though she liked him, she couldn't, she just couldn't, because she wasn't allowed a boyfriend, because it wasn't her culture or religion and it simply wasn't right or even possible.

She imagined trying to tell him about her Pakistani family, about her aloof father and her dominant mother, comparing it to what she knew about his artistic family and their house full of paintings and old books and their summers in the south of France, and it made her laugh with the absurdity of it all.

How could she explain, that her father barely knew her? That her mother still slapped her if she crossed a line? That she wasn't allowed home later than eight, and up until two years ago, she'd never really even spoken to a boy? That on weekends, her mother took her to meet women who might one day be her mother-in-law? It all sounded so ridiculous to say it out loud.

She fast-forwarded to the unimaginable, impossible scenario of bringing James home and she felt her brain explode, flickers of blinding light flashing before her eyes. She couldn't do this. She simply didn't know how.

She resolved to stay away from him. She ignored his texts and she tried.

But he was there, always there, with her coffee waiting and a seat saved before lectures, and he was there afterwards to walk with her and sit with her for hours.

He persisted. He talked to her incessantly in a way no one talked to her before. He held her gaze gently and she felt him considering her. When he said her eyes were pretty, finally, she believed him.

At night, Sara tossed and turned, staring across the space between her bed and her sister's. She wished she could stretch across the dark, speak wordlessly to Mariam and ask her, 'Are you happy? Do you dream of more than this too?'

But she knew that her older sister, who had never rebelled against their mother, never questioned their rules and still considered each and every suitor carefully, wouldn't approve. So Sara said nothing, while her mother kept shouting at her, for her short hair, for her cursed eyes and for the stubbornness that no one would want in a wife.

Sara did what she always did to block out the voice of her mother, and escaped into her collection of books. Every night, she read and reread, comforted by familiar words that had stayed with her since school days and never once wavered from the page.

She prayed, not on her prayer mat, but silently in her bed to her books, whispering, 'Give me strength.'

She turned to Jane Eyre and Mr Rochester and she concluded that she would not marry a Pakistani man picked by her mother from a pile of photos. She would not do what her mother expected. 'If I don't at least try, I will never live,' she thought. And Sara, seeing this one chance for the romance she dreamed of as a girl with a boy who was simply so kind, melted.

One afternoon, her hand slipped into his. James pulled her close and murmured, 'Finally,' in her ear.

For all of her life, ever since she was a child, Sara had lived two worlds divided.

At school she lived quietly in her imagination. When not required to pay attention in classes, she locked into the library among books where her friends were characters centuries old who spoke to her in top hats and empire line dresses.

At home, she lived in a tiny corner of her mother's Pakistan, where ever since she was a young girl she understood that one day, she would be married and this, the cooking, the cleaning, attending the mosque marriage committee meetings, is what she would do too. She understood, because it was what her mother did. She understood, because it was what she had always been told.

Her parents married over the phone, while her father was making his living in London and her mother was still in Lahore. Their wedding vows, each declaring their agreement to marry three times, were rushed down a crackling phone line. Sara's mother was 16 years old. She had never seen her husband before.

But Sara had never told anyone these things. At school, she never spoke of what she did at the weekend, of the family mosque trips when she'd change into shalwar kameez that made her feel self-conscious and unflattered or the segregated lunches with her mother's friends where there was no one, apart from Mariam, for her to talk to and nothing to do.

At university, she never quite committed to plans to go out, to see this play or hear that band. With Annie and her small group of girlfriends, she evaded over-dramatic conversations about long-distance ex-boyfriends or nights of regret spent with boys in their halls.

Nobody knew who she was, after eight o'clock in the evening, when she went home.

But with James, the two worlds she kept separate were dangerously colliding. She knew she could not keep pretending or start it all with a lie. As they inched closer and lay fingers entwined in quiet comfort, it was time for Sara to tell the truth.

'James,' she said quietly. 'There's things you don't know about me. There's things you need to know.'

It all tumbled out, one by one, punctuated by her voice breaking when it felt like too much to bear. She told him about her parents; her other way of life; her religion; her culture that didn't feel like it belonged to her but that was always, always there.

She told him about her mother's expectations, about the proposals she'd been receiving since she was a teenager and how she felt, with all seriousness and urgency, that as every year got closer to graduation, her time was running out.

She told him she had no more excuses to leave him every evening, but that, really, matter-of-factly, she just had to be home by eight. She told him there was nothing she could do about it. That there was nothing she could do about any of it.

'My family is not like your family,' she said. 'This will be hard. I am telling you now.'

James listened and Sara waited. She waited for confirmation. She waited for him to ask her to leave. She searched for a bemused, dismissive smile from a boy who had never had to fight or ask for anything in his life. But instead, he looked at her solemnly, the way she knew, deep down, that he would.

'Okay,' he said, his mind searching for answers that, right now, he couldn't find. 'I can't say I understand. But I can try. Let's just do this. Let's just try.' They had found each other, quickly and young, and each was a risk the other had to take.

It was, in some ways, an old-fashioned, coy courtship. There was no staying over, there were no photos shared with their friends online.

But the restraint on their relationship wasn't romantic. It shackled them to secrecy and, for the first time in her life, Sara set the rules. They would not kiss in public. They would not hold hands. James would not, could not, phone her after eight when she was at home.

On weekends, Sara used the library as an excuse to be out of the house, taking care to carry a tote bag with folders and books, then heading straight to James as soon as she slipped out.

But sometimes their weekend dates were cut short, interrupted by abrupt, inquisitive phone calls from her mother that she had to take, or cancelled completely by rushed, last-minute texts that said, 'I can't get out right now. Sorry.'

Once, an uncle bumped into them on their way to the cinema. James tried to reassure her. 'At least we weren't holding hands,' he said. But Sara couldn't stop panicking. A phone call from her mother quickly came, demanding she came home right now to explain. They abandoned their cinema tickets and their popcorn and James felt helpless, watching Sara run home to an interrogation where she had no choice but to lie, pretending he was only a boy from her course that she had just happened to bump into herself.

Her mother knew Sara was changing. Where once Sara had helped out at home, now she did so begrudgingly and with obvious resentment poured into extended sighs of exasperated indifference.

Sara had always been quiet at home, preferring her books to the television, but her mother noticed she had retreated even further. Where once Sara had sat with her mother on the sofa, and at the very least listened to her suggestions of suitors and good families to marry into, now she walked straight out of the room. When she called her downstairs, Sara ignored her, pretending she had to study instead.

Sara felt she was being watched. She slept with her phone under her pillow, terrified her mother would scroll through her messages, until finally, she decided to delete all of them, every single one, so not a trace of James remained.

She knew she had to be careful, and James told her repeatedly she could not let her anger show at home, but the more she was with him, the harder it was for her to accept the unfairness she felt.

For four years, Sara and James loved each other carefully wrapped in secrets and lies. It broke her heart, knowing that she could not love him openly.

For all the difficulties she had with her mother, deceit was not easy for her. It was hard, too, to keep James from Mariam. They did not spend all their time together now like they did when they were girls, but she longed to share both the burden and the beauty of her relationship with her sister. She longed to tell her that, maybe, just maybe, Mariam might find someone like James too. But Sara couldn't and it all was simply too much to bear.

'I don't like the person I am,' she told James, sadly. 'I don't know how much longer I can do this for.'

In their final year, Sara steeled herself for the end of their relationship. It hurt her to think of it but she forced herself to shake out of the daydream that had lasted, imperceptibly to her family, for years. She could not envisage it lasting. How could it? At university, they had the security of campus life that offered shelter from parents and uncles and aunts and prying family friends from the mosque. But outside of that world, how could they survive? Sara could see James slipping away.

Mariam had been working for two years now. She finished work at six o'clock, and her mother expected her sister home even earlier than eight now, sometimes reluctantly giving her leeway if the Tube was delayed. Mariam was likely to be engaged anytime soon, one particular family appearing more and more frequently for tea and lunch at their home. For Sara, it would be the same.

On graduation, she didn't ask her parents to come. She did not cheer for joy like the others. At the end of it, she walked away.

They tried. They tried for quick coffees after work, meeting in train stations and shop entrances. They snatched time and sent emails through work. Sometimes, they went weeks without seeing each other.

Sara phoned James on her walk home from the Tube station, sure to hang up before she unlocked the door. James talked optimistically of getting their own place, pretending to show Sara that everything really would be okay.

But she saw the exhaustion in his eyes and recognised the thickness in his voice that betrayed his own sadness. He had tried and she had tried and it felt like they had come as far as they could go.

'It's time,' said James, after yet another fraught meeting, frustrated at himself for not being able to do more to help ease the weight Sara carried with her all the time. 'It's time to tell the truth.'

It was not the wedding that either of them had hoped for. It was not a magical day.

They invited no friends and none of their favourite music was played. It was not the dress she had wanted and the invite did not even include his name.

But they were wed. They were wed, and it was over. At the end of the evening, James held Sara's hand, in front of her parents, and took her home. It was after eight o'clock and for the first time in four years, they could be alone.

It had not been easy. They had not expected it to. But from somewhere in among her sadness, Sara had found a tiny drop of strength that led her to find her mother in her bedroom late one night and sit down next to her and say, 'I've met a boy. I've met a boy I want to marry.'

When James asked Sara later what happened, she could not remember it right. It had blurred into a violent madness.

There was shouting. There was fury. There were fights and, once, Sara even felt her mother throw a punch. There was denial, there was outrage and then there were men, her father and her brothers, and all of them screaming over each other, 'No, never, no, a white boy, no, get out!'

Afterwards, there was silence. For weeks, Sara didn't speak. Mariam tried to talk to her. 'But what were you thinking?' she asked, gently.

Sara cut her hair even shorter, cropped close to her head now. She did not care. And then, she saw her mother weep. She had never seen her mother, the angry woman she had shoved away so many times, cry. But she sat there on the sofa, and she sobbed. Still, Sara did not go to her.

Her parents spoke first. They came to her with conditions. They would consider it, but only, only if this boy could prove certain things of standing, a good family background, a well-paid job, a place for Sara to live. That he would convert to Islam was indisputable. When, and only when, those conditions were met would they meet this boy. And then they would consider him.

For once, it was her father that spoke while her mother sat quietly, a part of her broken inside. It was not easy for them, but it was either this or lose Sara completely and they knew that now.

Hesitantly, James arrived into her parents' life. He spoke quietly but firmly. He stood for her father. His family overwhelmed hers with the general sense of positivity and happiness they always had about them. It startled Sara's parents but it also, somehow, made them feel less judged by the white English family that had come into their home and asked for their daughter's hand in marriage.

Later, Sara's mother knocked on her door and shyly showed her pictures, this time of elaborate Pakistani wedding gowns, lenghas with full-length silk skirts and dupattas edged in silver and gold. She silently offered her thick, heavy necklaces and earrings shaped like chandeliers.

They did not say sorry and still it hurt for words to come, but Sara accepted the tokens as what they were. 'I wanted only what was best for you,' her mother wanted to say, 'I wanted only to protect you. I tried but I failed. Forgive me, one day.'

Their wedding day was not easy. Sara's oldest brother refused to come. But with Mariam's help, her parents steadied themselves, smiling in photos and blessing their daughter in prayers.

Sara wore a white churidar first, a swinging dress worn over tight trousers with silver beads around the neck, and then changed into a lengha, a swishing silk skirt the colour of pistachios and rose petals. Her hair was still cropped short, and for a moment her mother reached out to touch it, but then lightly let her fingers brush Sara's cheek and stepped aside instead.

Sara and James have been married for nearly three years. They laugh now, when the clock nears eight and Sara does not have to disappear like Cinderella.

On the walls of their home, there are framed pictures of holidays and outings they no longer have to keep hidden and there are even some that James, a keen photographer, has taken of Sara alone. Sara does not mind having her picture taken now. She smiles in every one.

It took a long while for her mother to understand his ways, this boy her daughter married who still looks so young. But she watches him look after her.

He likes to cook, which her mother finds amusing for she has not known a boy to enjoy cooking in the kitchen before, but she passes along her recipes for homemade naans and curries nevertheless. She wonders if Mariam will find a boy like this, who is kind and gentle and helpful too, and decides that if she did, it would, perhaps, not be so bad.

There are still scars between Sara and her mother. They have not flawlessly healed and perhaps they never completely will. But for now, Sara comes home sometimes and helps lay the table and it is not quite silent between them.

4

Within four walls

Vinu had lost count of how many times he had asked Kalpesh if he would come to Reema's wedding. He had tried persuading him and coaxing him in various ways but still, Kalpesh said no, refusing to listen. 'But she is your sister,' said Vinu. 'How can you say no?'

Kalpesh, however, had been counting exactly how many times the subject of Reema's wedding had come up in recent conversation. He noted, silently in his head, that his father had already asked him fifteen times in four days to consider going to it. He wondered how many more conversations about it they would need.

Vinu had tried his best to reassure Kalpesh that the wedding would be bearable. He promised him that they would only stay for two hours and that he did not have to go in the coach and its unfamiliar, itchy upholstered seats and anonymous finger smears on the windows with the other guests. Instead Vinu said he would drive him there himself. Still, Kalpesh refused.

Charu was worried about what the groom's family would say, muttering that she had enough to think about being the mother-of-the-bride. She wondered how they would explain their eldest and only son's absence on their daughter's wedding day. Even though they had not taken him to any of their Gujarati gatherings over the past year, Vinu and Charu both felt it would be better for Kalpesh to come to Reema's wedding than to make up excuses about him instead.

Charu tried too. She promised Kalpesh that she would prepare his meal herself and take it with her in one of the sets of matching tupperware boxes she had designated for his food. She offered to wash his plates and cutlery herself in boiling hot water, just as she did for him at home, and promised to lay his place at one of the family's reserved tables, although she worried it might cause their guests to gossip about her son's strange requests. Kalpesh listened to his mother, but still he said nothing at all.

Reema promised him nothing. She had seen her parents try with desperation in their different ways and she had seen her brother stare blankly all the while, blocking out their voices in his head and imagining he was somewhere else instead even though he never went anywhere at all.

It had made her cry. She cried quietly in her room, allowing herself for a brief moment to feel pained and hurt and angry that her older brother could not even try to be there. But she dried her tears quickly, chiding herself for blaming him, which she had never done before, as she knew none of it was his fault. Eventually, she simply asked him one final time, palms upturned and eyes large and moist with tears, to be there on her wedding day because she needed him.

Though she could not be sure, she thought she moved Kalpesh in some inscrutable way that day, brushing him with her careful, open words as gently as the floating white dandelion seeds they used to chase together as children when Kalpesh's life was not regulated by routines or, at least, not as much.

Vinu was not sure whether it was Reema's words, or Charu's or his, but on the morning of Reema's wedding, Kalpesh stood in the hallway, looking distracted and awkward and fidgety. 'I want to come,' he said. He had showered, seven times already. He had been in the bathroom since early morning. He was ready.

Vinu tried not to show Kalpesh how relieved and pleased he was for he knew it was best not to turn the significance of this step, as the psychiatrist often said, into something else. But it was all he could do not to grab his son in an embrace. It had been so long since he had held him.

Instead Vinu nodded, affecting calm while inside him a seed of hope that had long lain buried and latent beneath the layered burdens of family life suddenly bloomed and surged and Vinu could not escape the thought that, perhaps, this meant Kalpesh was getting better after all.

But as soon he had formed the thought, he pushed it forcefully out of his mind. He could not let himself think about that, not today. Today was Reema's day and Vinu knew it had been a long time since she came first.

He whispered quickly in Charu's ear, telling her Kalpesh had decided to come, speaking softly in Gujarati so Kalpesh would not hear. Her eyes sparkled with surprise like the diamantes studded all over her sari, before she hurriedly went to the kitchen to carefully spoon rice and lentils into tupperware boxes as she had promised, for she did not want Kalpesh to worry about caterers he did not know touching his food.

Kalpesh stayed upstairs in his room while the wedding guests arrived, parking their shiny cars messily over pavements, bumper to bumper, congregating to take their seats in the coach that Vinu had organised to take them to the wedding hall. Downstairs, he could hear the toilet flushing and the bathroom taps running every few minutes as guests prepared themselves last minute for the hour-long journey to Leicester.

He clenched his jaw and tried not to imagine the water drops in the sink or the hand towel, damp and misaligned on the rail, left by their guests washing their hands carelessly. He tried not to consider the heavy smell of thick perfume and stale aftershave and dull sweat, which he imagined coated each guest's strands of hair and filled their every pore, mixing in the bathroom air and leaving an imprint of all of the people who had been in there. He tried to think about his psychologist's technique of shifting his focus, but it was hard to concentrate, with all those people downstairs. He wondered whether it was a good idea to go to the wedding after all. It was thirty-seven minutes before his father called up the stairs, saying it was time to leave.

In the car, Kalpesh was quiet. Vinu wondered what he was thinking about, but knew it was best not to ask. Kalpesh never spoke much anyway, offering monosyllabic answers to questions instead. It had been a year since the diagnosis, and since then Vinu and Charu had taken care not to take Kalpesh to noisy, chattering Indian social events, telling people he was busy or had gone somewhere or was not in the mood for socialising, shrugging their shoulders while giving short, fixed smiles as if to say, 'These children, what can you do?'

But, really, they were afraid of what people might think or what people would say. In India, people did not talk about these things, or if they did it was with a sneer, deriding someone like Kalpesh as mad, pagal, when really it was not that at all. So Vinu and Charu told Reema not to talk about Kalpesh and his problems outside of their home. 'It is our affair,' they said. 'We keep it within our four walls. Nobody needs to know.'

It was best, they thought, to keep this to themselves although, still, they worried that the news would escape. Kalpesh had long ago left work, unable to cope, and the hospital appointments were long and draining and confusing and only when it got too much to bear did they tell Vinu's sisters whom they felt they could trust.

When Kalpesh was first diagnosed, Charu could not understand it and Vinu felt as if he should have known, as if he had missed something while Kalpesh was growing up. It had been a terrible year of bewilderment and tears and sadness as they confronted the scientific facts presented to them.

But Reema's wedding had brought them happiness, tinged with an unspoken relief that Kalpesh's condition had not affected her prospects. The wedding was something to look forward to and it gave them something else to plan other than hospital appointments with countless psychiatrists and psychologists and, as he drove, Vinu prayed that today would be a good day.

When they arrived, Charu rushed to the bridal suite where Reema was getting ready while Vinu ushered Kalpesh quickly in, conscious of him flinching at the professional photographer's flash for he did not like having his picture taken.

Kalpesh chose to sit alone at the wedding, selecting the one reserved family table that was not filled. At first people did not notice him, too distracted by the trays of samosas and spring rolls being offered as canapes and, later, the entrance of the bride and groom. But gradually, after the ceremonies when people began to chat, a few old acquaintances went over to greet him and to ask him where he had been all year.

Kalpesh shrugged abruptly and answered briefly and fidgeted with his hands and his knees. Those who spoke to him exchanged bemused looks. 'He has always been weird,' said some of the guests to each other, who tried and failed to make conversation with him.

Vinu was nervous. Though he had hoped Kalpesh would come, he had not really expected him to and so had not planned properly what to do. When it was time to eat, Vinu watched Charu slip away into the wedding hall's kitchen, carrying out scalding hot crockery and smudgeless cutlery from the kitchen to set at Kalpesh's place, trying discreetly to tip the contents of the reheated tupperware boxes she had brought with her in a plastic bag onto his plate.

As Vinu looked around the hall, he noticed people watching, confused at what Charu was doing. He began to wish they had not continually pressed Kalpesh to come. Inexplicably, he felt a protective fury inside him rising fast and hot and threatening to spill over like the running water Kalpesh used to fill the bathroom sink and wash his hands with hundreds of times a day, and Vinu began to wonder why he and Charu had invited the majority of the people in the room.

But it was Reema's wedding day, Vinu reminded himself, and there were guests to greet and ceremonies to sit through and formal photographs to sit for on the stage. He had neither time nor opportunity to keep checking on Kalpesh, who was growing more and more anxious about the time.

When finally Vinu broke away to go to him, Kalpesh was sitting fidgeting with the watch on his wrist and his hands and his knees, looking exasperated and frustrated and impatient.

'You said we would stay two hours, Papa,' he said, louder than was necessary. 'It has been nearly three and a half. We have to go. You promised. You said.'

He insisted they leave immediately, shaking his head furiously as he always did to signify the end of a conversation he was unhappy with.

As Vinu tried to reason with him, Kalpesh's anger grew and he began shouting louder over the music beating through the speakers and the chattering of the guests. He shouted about promises and about keeping to time and that he was tired. Guests, who were already curious about why the brother of the bride was sitting alone, turned to stare.

Reema, who had told her new husband about Kalpesh when they were engaged but had so hoped for him not to see her brother this way, dropped her smile distractedly as she heard the commotion and did not hear the photographer calling for her to tilt her head and shift her gaze.

Vinu's sisters gathered quickly round and Charu touched Kalpesh's arm lightly with her fingers but he shoved her aside roughly, enough for her to stumble startled over her sari and accidentally tip a few frail glasses off the table and onto the floor. As the guests gasped and the glasses fell like long-stemmed roses tumbling in slow motion and Reema rushed unthinkingly to her mother's side to help her back onto her feet, Vinu realised they should not have pressed Kalpesh to come at all.

Finally when they somehow calmed him down enough to walk out of the wedding hall and sit in the car, Kalpesh sat in a silence that was cold and aggressive and heavy with blame and it shrouded Vinu in shame. As they drove home, Vinu wanted to reach over and put an arm around Kalpesh or place his own withered hand over his sons and promise he would never have to go to these functions ever again. He wanted to apologise for persuading him to come, when he had said all along that he had not wanted to. 'I am sorry,' he wanted to say. 'How can I make things better for you, my son?'

But Vinu and Kalpesh did not talk like this. They did not talk about feelings and forgiveness and sorrow and love and guilt. They never did, even before the diagnosis.

It was not the first time Kalpesh had rapidly lost control of his temper, but on Reema's wedding day, it had been somewhat harder for Vinu to bear. He was glad to see his daughter settled but somewhere inside he longed desperately for the same for his eldest child, his only son.

Yet he knew it was a distant vanishing hope, floating like the tiny flecks of suspended dust Kalpesh frequently complained about that could be seen only in sunlight, for just a second, and then lightly disappeared as if they had never been there at all.

And so, they sat in silence in the car on the journey back from the wedding. The words Vinu longed to say lodged in his throat, stale and dry, only later dissolving into sad and quiet and breathless tears which he shed alone, after Kalpesh went to his room and before the wedding coach full of its loud gossiping guests, who had been well fed by the caterers paid for by Vinu's wallet, returned home.

It only took days after the wedding for the news to spread among the network of Gujarati families that they knew, passed along in whispers that contorted along the way elaborately like the slowly fading bridal henna painted on Reema's hands flowing from her palms in different directions.

Vinu's sisters tried to dispel the gossip and prevent Vinu and Charu from hearing it, but it was in vain. 'Have you heard? Vinu's son has gone pagal!' the cruel rumours went. 'He pushed his mother over! He does not speak! He does strange, strange things!' Some rumours were meaner, colder, sterner, blaming Vinu and Charu for neglecting Kalpesh and causing his brain to turn crazed.

Vinu was numbed by what he heard. He was stung by the readiness of those he had considered long-time family friends to talk with thoughtless and tactless tongues about his family's misfortune, speculating about his son excitedly and wildly as if they had nothing else to do.

He had known some of them as a young man in India, before they had each come to England in turn. They had been each other's brothers, each other's family, a long way from home. Their wives had turned to each other in the absence of sisters and mothers and female cousins, sharing recipes and household tips and talking of how things were done differently in England. Their children had grown up sharing clothes and school books and toys. They celebrated special occasions and they held onto their memories of home together through pujas and trips to the temple and talking in their mother tongue. So how, then, could they talk about Kalpesh in this way?

But Vinu realised, as he heard the things that were being said among his circle, that the bond between them was breaking. He realised, bitterly and disillusioned, that somehow his Gujarati friends had become more concerned with competing with each other for status than caring for each other in times of need.

As Charu sobbed in the bathroom, wounded by the twisted words about her family that she had heard, and Kalpesh stayed for days at a time in his room unknowing, Vinu felt deeply hurt and isolated. Slowly, the phone calls inviting them to dinner or tea at this or that family's house came less and less frequently, and on the rare occasions that they did, Vinu and Charu meekly refused, preferring to stay at home instead. Nobody wanted to talk to them, the family with the mad, pagal, son.

Reema had long gone to her husband's house now, and Vinu and Charu spent their days alone in their home, looking for ways to care for Kalpesh. They drove him to appointments at hospitals and clinics and organised home visits. They helped him with exercises he was given to do, like writing down the number of times he washed his hands or checked the house's windows and doors in the journal his psychiatrist had provided, the pages of which Kalpesh would not turn himself. This was how their days passed.

Sometimes, Vinu's sisters came bringing with them helpful offerings of food, or bags of supermarket shopping which Charu, who was so busy with Kalpesh's requests, had not always the time to do. Vinu thought it a blessing that his retirement had come so soon so that he could care for Kalpesh too.

Meanwhile Vinu wondered if perhaps the signs had always been there. Had Kalpesh always been like this? Vinu turned the question over in his mind, again and again, late at night in his study while looking at old family photographs, searching for clues.

Kalpesh had been a quiet child, preferring mostly to be on his own. He shunned the playground for their simple, square suburban garden where he drew numbers on the patio or lined toy cars up all in a row. He did not seek affection but he was quiet and no bother and both Vinu and Charu thought him a perfect child.

As he grew older, he grew quieter still, preferring his books and numbers and sheets of papers covered in equations that spoke to him more than everyday conversation did. Charu called him her thoughtful boy. 'He is always thinking,' she said.

When Kalpesh reached sixth form, the headmaster called Vinu in. Kalpesh's grades were excellent, yes, but he was increasingly difficult in class. Sometimes he was deliberately obnoxious in his offhand mannerisms, and he did not participate in groups. Though Vinu listened, he did not think of this as exceptionally odd. A little impolite, perhaps, but not odd, not strange. That was just the way Kalpesh was, Vinu thought, and he felt the headmaster was wrong. He was pleased with his bookish boy and his solitary intelligence and content that he did not waste his time on football or parties like other boys at school.

So even when Kalpesh answered in monosyllables, or locked himself in the bathroom for hours or stayed up all night tiptoeing through the house, Vinu was not concerned. At mealtimes, when he refused to eat food which was not steaming or moaned about things like dishes covered in cling film, they simply thought he was being picky. 'Teenagers,' Vinu said to Charu, whenever she complained. But now after every hospital appointment, Vinu could not help but look back and wonder with regret. If only they had noticed.

It had got worse after school. At first Kalpesh had resisted university despite winning a top place. But Vinu laughed as if the idea of not going was entirely absurd, and strongly refused to entertain such talk again. Kalpesh lived at home and travelled to his classes but frequently he skipped them saying he already knew the subjects at hand. Vinu could not insist as Kalpesh's grades were indeed excellent, but it was only now that he realised that Kalpesh was simply avoiding taking the train, a public, crowded space smeared with other people's fingerprints, smudged by other people's breath, and the unknown, unfamiliar places that did not feel right to him.

It was the same with work. Kalpesh asked for a year out upon graduating to stay at home but Vinu brushed his talk off as nonsense. 'You are clever, you are capable, but why are you so lazy?' he once shouted. It was Vinu who insisted, printing off applications for top corporate jobs, picturing his son making money in the Square Mile. It was Vinu who raised his voice, offering Kalpesh no choice.

It was only after Kalpesh returned early from work one day, just three weeks in, and refused to go back and they fought for hours that Reema, who had previously never interrupted Vinu when he shouted like this, broke into Kalpesh's room.

'You always push him, Papa,' she said, for the first time in her life lifting her voice at her parents, her words thick and dry and breaking. 'Why can't you see that something's wrong? Haven't you noticed the way he is changing? He is scared. He is so scared, and you just can't see!'

For several painful days the house was robbed of the familiar and comforting humdrum of each family member's footfall and daily routine, as they picked their way about stealthily. Reema avoided Vinu and Vinu avoided Kalpesh and Charu was stuck desperately in between.

Eventually Reema came to Vinu one night as he sat in his study, poring over bank account statements and bills, the way he always did when he needed to be on his own, and she handed him a bundle of A4 sheets.

There were words she had highlighted, like 'anxiety' and 'debilitating' and 'impulses' and 'routine'. There were passages she had underlined, like 'interferes with the ability to function' and 'avoidance of places' and 'can have a totally devastating impact on a person's entire life.' She sat quietly while Vinu read and then turned to her, his face confused and crumpled as she reached out for his hand.

Since Reema had left home, there was a stillness in the house and it lingered in thick layers like invisible dust as the years passed. Vinu and Charu had fallen out of contact with many of their former friends since the gossip that had spread in the aftermath of Reema's wedding, and although Charu insisted she did not need such spitefulness in her life, replacing friends with prayer, Vinu knew she missed her routine and the liveliness which the variety of different company could bring. They did not go anywhere now.

Vinu noticed Charu slowing down. Every day she spent hours at the stove cooking fresh food for Kalpesh, storing it in separate containers and serving it on separate plates as he would not eat out of anything else, and it was wearing her out. They were older now, and Kalpesh was older too, and things were slower, harder and more challenging to do.

Charu cried frequently and when Vinu asked why she simply shook her head, unable to speak, as if she might burst from taking a breath, as if the weight of life alone was too much to bear. She worried constantly and Vinu prayed that if anything were to happen that she should go first, please, for he could not leave her behind like this.

Sometimes Vinu felt that ever since the diagnosis, which seemed so long ago, Kalpesh had grown worse not better. It was hard to convince Kalpesh to leave the house, where he sat all day with the television on or carried out his checks and his routines. When his psychiatrists toyed with his levels of medication, Kalpesh suffered turbulent fits and each time was frightening and horrendous to bear. Each time, Vinu held his breath and fought back his tears and prayed silently, rocking slowly in a tiny movement back and forth.

It seemed as if every day there were more and more things Kalpesh would not do, like open the fridge door or touch the microwave or eat fruit with his fingers or pick up the phone and it was all up to Charu and Vinu to do. It took some time for Vinu to realise that Kalpesh would rather go hungry than touch a cupboard handle to take out a plate.

He started asking them to do unusual things too, like polish their house keys clean with antibacterial wipes as soon as they stepped through the door, or tip breakfast cereal into plastic containers and throw the cardboard boxes away. He panicked if the doorbell rang unexpectedly, with a look on his face so terrible and so frightened that Vinu wanted only to stroke his hair, so thin now, and tell him everything was okay.

They lived like this for seven slow years before the psychiatrist suggested that Kalpesh move out and live on his own. Charu cried and Vinu positioned a frail arm around her, both of them shocked at the advice.

Neither of them had ever considered sending their son to live alone; it was not something they could ever do. 'We are not like English families, our children do not move out,' Vinu said shyly. 'We cannot send our son away on his own.' Even during their time at university, both children lived at home, he explained, and Reema left only after marriage. Kalpesh had not been apart from them for even one night.

The psychiatrist listened, understanding and patient, but he pointed to Charu's growing stress and said he felt it was for the best, that it was too much for them both on their own, that Kalpesh might make more progress alone. It had been seven years now and Kalpesh's advances had been slow. Vinu and Charu had been unable to break away from participating in his routines which, the psychiatrist gently said, was making things harder.

He reminded them Kalpesh was still struggling with simple coping techniques, unable to list the number of times he washed his hands or checked the door because he still did not touch the pad of paper or the pen he was given to keep.

It would be difficult at first, but it could help. They would find him a flat nearby, with the council's help. It was an option, he said, but one they should consider, that was all.

'He thinks we have failed our son,' said Charu, quietly in the car. 'It is what they all think.' It was the only thing she said that day.

Later that night, while Charu was asleep, breathing fitfully, Vinu heard Kalpesh walking around the house as he still did late at night. He walked, from room to room, from the family bathroom upstairs to the shower room downstairs and back again, checking, locking, turning taps on, washing and washing again.

Vinu lay there and he listened and he looked across at Charu, her face lined with worry and her forehead rumpled even in sleep and worn not just from age but from the fears she carried inside, and he felt that he could not bear it if she were to break from the heaviness of it all.

It was surprising, how Kalpesh accepted the proposal to live on his own. Vinu did not know what the psychiatrist had said to him, but he suspected Kalpesh felt it would be easier to be by himself, to no longer hide his habits for no one would be there all the time to see. The flat the council found was small and clean, a short drive away. There were carers to help from the day centre nearby and Vinu began to feel that this was a good thing, after all.

It was harder for Charu. She felt she had let her son down. She felt it was wrong for strangers to care for him. 'It is not what we do,' she insisted, her weathered hands in tight, tiny fists battling gently against his chest as she broke down. Vinu said nothing but held her, and he clung to the hope that this decision was best.

It has been nearly fifteen years since Kalpesh moved out on his own. Vinu and Charu visit every day and Charu still cooks him his separate food in his separate containers although sometimes, Kalpesh makes himself a sandwich or two, provided that day he is capable of opening the fridge door.

Reema visits often and when she does, she confronts Kalpesh, playful and lively in a way the psychiatrist agrees is good for him. She crosses her arms and refuses to open cupboards he still will not touch or heat up his food and insists she will not leave until he does it himself, like the bossy little sister she always was.

Kalpesh's moods are not so extreme now, and he laughs sometimes too. He is distant with his nephew and his niece, and Reema is careful the children never stay long. But there are moments when Kalpesh might smile or give a hint of something – which is not quite happiness but is nearly – away and Vinu and Charu and Reema notice and think to themselves in the language of the psychiatrists they have heard over the years that, yes, that is a significant step indeed.

Charu's nerves are less fraught now. She prays every day for hours and it gives her peace. In what was once Kalpesh's bedroom, she has made a shrine, a small altar and statues of deities, and that is her own ritual now. At the temple, she has made a small circle of new friends and she is not so alone, and though she still sometimes wakes in the night from sudden panic like a fearful child, she turns to Vinu and he calms her down.

Vinu is an old man. He is thinner and frailer and walks much more slowly now. He looks smaller and his joints are creaky and stiff, and though he worries about Charu and Kalpesh and the future and what it may bring, he is accepting of it. He prays alongside Charu, seeing the strength it gives, and he believes the future is in the hands of the gods now.

Vinu is no longer worried about what people in their Gujarati circle might think as he was when Kalpesh was first diagnosed, when together with Charu he decided not to tell anyone anything. He is not ashamed of his son.

When he passes old acquaintances and those friends who distanced themselves from his family and grew apart from him in the street, he explains that his son is not mad, not pagal, but suffers simply from biik, from phobia and fear, and that he is doing so much better now.

There are many things Vinu wishes he could give Kalpesh, things he had always imagined his son would obtain; a family of his own, a wife, a good home and an easier life, rich and full without the sharp painful stabs of anxiety which his son still sometimes deals with. He wishes he could offer all of these things to his son, one by one, like wrapped-up gifts for him to unfold and treasure forever. He wishes he could tell Kalpesh that he prays for all these things for him every day.

There are days that helplessness causes Vinu overwhelming grief, but there are also days he holds onto hope. And there are days, too, when Vinu visits Kalpesh, and although still they do not talk about feelings and forgiveness and sorrow and love and guilt, and although still there is so much that Vinu would like to say to his son, they sit quietly on the sofa with the television on, side by side, and in these moments, life feels normal again.

5

Teen

She is 13, and she hates herself. She has hair in all the wrong places. It is on her face and her arms and her legs and her stomach, little black hairs that lie flat and lined up in parallel, making her look like she has been sewn together with a closely placed running stitch, up and down.

In the changing rooms at school, the hair on her legs, dark and dense, marks her out. The other girls in her class have clean skin all over or, if they have any hair on their legs or their arms at all, it is soft and scant, feathery and golden.

The only visible blemishes these girls have are love bites on their necks from their beginner boyfriends who go to the boys' grammar school next door.

Sometimes, they complain about them, wondering how to hide them underneath the collar of their school shirts. She does not know how these love bites, tiny purple shadows of abject passion, appear but one day she looks them up in secret on the dial-up Internet they have recently installed at home. It is highly unlikely, she thinks, that she will ever face the conundrum of having to hide one herself.

On Tuesdays, they have swimming. She hates it. There are no curtains across the cubicles so she hides in the toilet so that she can get changed, emerging at the very last second just as their class is about to start.

One morning while getting dressed for school, she realises she can wear her swimsuit under her uniform and then perhaps not worry so much about removing her clothes. She wonders why it took her so long to come up with this particular brainwave. Still, it does not solve everything.

Though the sight of them is slightly blurred by the water, everyone can still see her legs. She still has to hear the other girls laugh and call her names as she desperately tries to cover up with her towel and her thick black tights.

She notices some of the girls stare at her upper lip on the rare occasions they talk to her, so she starts to part her hair so it falls across the front of her face in an attempt to hide behind it. She constantly has to brush her hair out of her eyes but she knows no other option, so it will have to do. Once, one of the more popular girls held a hand to her chin and with some force pushed her head back against the wall, saying she would bring in a razor and do it herself if she did not sort it out soon. A teacher overheard, and ordered a lunchtime detention. 'It is unacceptable,' the teacher said. 'Her culture is different and you cannot behave that way.'

She is relieved the teacher has stepped in. But she is not sure what any of it has to do with her culture; she wonders what that even means, anyway.

In winter, they play hockey. Although it is bitterly cold, school policy insists they wear their short gym skirts, pleated across the front and buttoned at the side. It is the early 1990s, a time before Pakistanis and Muslims are at the centre of the news, so things like guidelines for inclusiveness at schools for pupils of different faiths do not yet exist at her girls school. Though her parents are not happy about it, it has not occurred to them that they might claim religious exemption from the rules. So she continues to wear it; it is the only short skirt she owns.

She is relieved that they must also wear knee-high socks, pulled straight over their shinpads, but her relief has little to do with any sense of modesty. The socks at least cover her calves, where for some reason the hair is blacker and sharper than elsewhere, wiry like small spiders' legs crawling all over her skin.

But in the changing rooms afterwards, as she sits half frozen in the corner, waiting for her hands to melt so that she can move her fingers and put on the rest of her clothes, she looks down at her chafed thighs and is horrified by what she sees.

Her thighs are sore and pimpled from the cold, the downy dark hair standing up as if waving for her attention, and she wonders with curious detachment whether these legs that are so violently ugly belong to her at all. 'Is it because of your religion?' ask her classmates, with looks of pity but mostly mild disgust. 'Is that why you can't shave your legs?'

Honestly, she does not know. So she asks her mother later that night if it is haram, is that why she is not allowed to remove it, but her mother just tells her off instead.

'Silly girl,' she says, 'we are not Sikh, don't you know anything about your religion and your culture at all?'

Not really, she thinks with sincerity. She has never been told why they do things a certain way at home, only that they just do. She knows there is a black list of all the things she cannot and will not ever do, like go out with boys or drink or eat pork or smoke, but it is never explained to her why.

'It is our religion. It is our culture. It is the way we do things,' her parents always say on the rare occasions she asks.

She strokes the hair on her forearm and waits for an explanation now, but her mother does not offer one and says instead huffily that she is too young to think of these things and should not be concerned with what the English girls think. They only shave their legs to show them off and shamelessly tempt boys, her mother says. Other than her games lessons, her legs should be covered and not seen. That, her mother says, is the end of it.

'But it's embarrassing,' she wants to say. 'Please, don't make me go to school like this,' she pleads in her head. 'You have not heard the names they say.'

Sometimes, when she is alone in the bathroom and behind the privacy of a locked door she picks up her father's razor and examines it in her hand. She wonders what would happen if she scraped it against her skin. Curious, she tries it every now and again on a small patch above her ankle, daring to inch higher along her calf. But her skin is too dry and the blade grates against her tawny flesh so that every time she drags it, little spots of blood scrabble to the surface, bubbles about to burst.

She is 14, nearly 15. She still hates herself. All the other girls in her school have pretty names like the characters in the books she likes to read. They are all Charlottes and Beths, Amys and Sophies, Elizabeths and Claires.

Everyone makes fun of her name, because they say it the wrong way. At first when she had just started senior school, it began with her teachers.

'I thought your people didn't drink,' her class tutor said while going through the register on the first day of school.

'Do your parents like a tipple?' asked another, with a wry smile.

She remained stony-faced but also too shy to reply, not quite sure of what point they were trying to make. She tries to tell them they are not pronouncing it right but because they are busy working their way through the class register they do not listen, or if they do, it makes no difference to them at all.

Now that they are older and more aware of other jokes to be made at her expense, some of the girls in her year have begun to mock her name too. 'Are you pissed?' they cackle, pushing into her with their shoulders in the corridors, forcing her to lose her balance.

In several years from now, she will learn to accept the subtle beauty of her first name. She will introduce herself to strangers with a smile and she will tell them even when they do not ask that it means the sweet fragrance of rose petals, before anyone has the chance to quip anything else at all.

By the time she is in her late twenties, she will meet several men via an online Asian matrimonial site and when she is about to give up in despair, one of them will send her a snappy private message referencing the meaning of her name and the roses he likes to cultivate in his spare time and because of this unusual hobby and unusual connection, she agrees to give him a chance. When months later they are engaged, he will send her roses because of it, buy her expensive bottles of exquisite rose perfume for Valentine's Day because he says it reminds him of her and of her name.

On their wedding night, 20 years from now, he will scatter thick petals the size of thumbprints across their pillows and because roses means something else to them, because they symbolise her name, she does not think the gesture is clichéd.

When she is at work, she will stress the traditional Arabic intonation so that her name sounds like a word that might end a line in an ancient love poem. Her clients will always tell her she has a lovely name, an unusual name. They will frequently ask her where it comes from and she will explain her Pakistani heritage to them succinctly with a pride she never possessed as a teenager before expertly steering the conversation back to the details of their legal case.

And although it will annoy her that one of her colleagues will insist on constantly mispronouncing her name despite it being so easy, really, she will continue to correct him tirelessly again and again.

But right now, because she is about to turn 15, she hates her name. The rest of the girls in her class spend their Saturday nights at house parties with the boys from the school next door, where they do things like drink bottles from their parents' stash and kiss and grope in the dark, and they find it hilarious that her name is Abeer.

'Fancy A Beer? Can I get you A Beer?' the boys from the school next door shout to each other making lewd gestures that intend to reduce her further in some way.

It is crueller still, because it is not just her name they are making fun of but the rest of her too, as though the idea of finding her even remotely attractive is so utterly absurd. She convinces herself that if it were not for her name, they would not notice her at all and she would just be the brown-skinned girl, although, really, there would be hundreds of other things for them to bully her about, like the fact that she is from Pakistan and she has hair on her face and her arms and her legs. She walks to the bus stop with her head down, pretending not to hear, while the girls in her year look on and laugh, all high-pitched and pony-tailed.

'Why?' she asks her parents, raging against them, wondering how they could be so stupid. 'Why would you ever think it was a good idea to call me this? We live in England for God's sake. *Everyone* drinks. I am stuck with this, for the rest of my life.'

But her parents insist it is a beautiful name. It is the name of her father's sister who died long before she was born. It is an honour to preserve her memory, it is a good Pakistani name, they say.

'Would you rather we had called you Poppy or Tanya, or some other English-sounding name that has little to do with your culture, like Anglicised Indian parents do?'

It's not even a Pakistani name, she thinks silently. 'It's Arabic, you fools,' she says to them in her mind.

They shout at her, telling her that they did not raise her to be ashamed of who she is. But she is. Right now, she is.

After school, Abeer closes her bedroom door and turns the pages of the thin, shiny magazines she has started to buy. The magazines tell her how to wear glitter eyeshadows and not to kiss while wearing lipgloss and what to do the morning after if she should ever go too far, things that it is unlikely she will ever need to know.

But these are the magazines she sees the other girls reading at school, slipping them inside their ring binders whenever a teacher comes near, and Abeer thinks that by reading the same magazines as them, she might learn how to be like them too.

Abeer buys her magazines from the newsagent's she passes on the way back from school and hides her copies at home on a shelf above her desk where she is supposed to do her homework, tightly slotted between the multicoloured covers of her children's encyclopedia set given to her by her uncle as a gift for passing her eleven-plus.

Her mother, who stretches out her leggings after washing them so that they fit saggy and loose and not skintight as intended and only buys her tops that are long enough to reach her thighs, would be furious if she knew.

Knowing this thrills Abeer. But even though she feels victorious against her mother, buying these magazines with the money she is given for emergencies, snacks and lunch, each page she reads peels away a little layer of her without her even noticing it.

She likes looking through these magazines, at the clothes and the boy band posters and the agony aunt pages and the relationship tips, but they also leave her feeling empty, and often when she is done with this or that issue she lies on her bed on her back feeling fed up and frumpy. Everyone inside her magazines is pretty and popular and blonde, smooth-legged and flat-stomached.

She, on the other hand, has eyebrows that meet in the middle and an outline of sideburns down her face and, to her horror, a little rim has popped out around her middle which her mother and her aunts tease her endlessly about.

She does not see herself in these magazines. She keeps reading them, but they remind her that she is different to the other girls at school. These magazines keep taunting her, telling her she is not beautiful and that she cannot ever be.

She will continue to feel this way for years, even when she is in her early twenties and all her body hair is whipped off by hot wax like clockwork magic.

At university she will lie on her bed in her halls of residence and will flick through piles of glossy magazines with her best friend, whose parents are from Sri Lanka, and together they will sigh, exasperated and deflated by glossy pictures of beautiful and pale and thin women they know they will never look like, always wondering why they waste their money on these things.

Sometimes they will debate seriously, question why there are never ethnic models on the front covers of fashion magazines and then they will collapse into laughter because they just referred to themselves as ethnic, before swearing to each other again and again that they will boycott these publications until the following month, when one of them invariably caves.

When she is alone, she will roll her eyes at her reflection in the mirror, remind herself that she is intelligent and is one day going to be a lawyer, for crying out loud, and while she is at it, she will also remind herself that she is not that ugly any more either.

By the time she has left university and started work as a trainee solicitor, she will have taken great steps to improve her looks. She will frequently assess herself and try to see the positive things, like how her sandy-coloured and now hair-free skin is unblemished and smooth and how her eyes are glossy and deep like puddles of melted chocolate.

She will keep telling herself she has assets in her appearance after all but it is not until she is engaged to be married that she finally accepts her looks and acknowledges she really is quite attractive anyway.

But right now, because she is 15, she simply feels inadequate in every way. She wonders what it would be like to wake up and look pretty in the morning and she thinks she would give anything to feel that way. Her mother once told her Allah answers everything they pray for, so she starts to pray in all earnest for her face to change.

She is aware that it is not all bad; she is frequently commended by her female relatives for the colour of her skin, which is lightly tanned and not too dark. When she is older, people will be surprised when they ask her where she is from and she tells them Pakistan. 'But you don't look it at all,' they exclaim. 'You could be Spanish!' as if they are offering her a compliment.

But as a teenager she hates the colour of her skin which is neither fair nor dark, because it shows up all of the hair she hates. At least if she were darker, she thinks, she would be able to hide it.

She buys facial bleach from the high street chemist and mixes it with white powder stiff and shiny like whipped meringues, then dabs it under her nose. It stings and, because she leaves it on longer than necessary just to be sure it will work, it makes her skin angry. She comes out of the bathroom crying. Her tears alarm her mother, and though she is annoyed with Abeer for what she has done, she soothes her skin with neem oil dabbed on soft cotton wool until the harsh, bleached patches calm down.

But her mother's sympathy does not last long. She is worried Abeer is becoming too English, because she thinks she is starting to show an attitude. She calls her gori, in a critical way, and starts to insist that Abeer change out of her school uniform and into shalwar kameez every night and on weekends too. Abeer refuses. She does not understand the point of it.

'What difference does it make, what clothes I wear?'

'It is your culture. It is so that you do not forget.'

'How can I forget something I don't even know?'

It continues, the sniping and the snapping back and forth. They argue over everything. For three weeks, they do not talk to each other directly because her mother insists Abeer should speak Urdu at home but Abeer refuses, until eventually her mother reverts back to speaking in English again.

Abeer starts to slam her bedroom door causing her mother to despair, turning to her father in tears and blaming him for the way Abeer is turning out, saying that this would never have happened if she had been brought up in Pakistan where they belonged.

'Oh, because teenagers there are so perfect,' Abeer thinks sarcastically, slumped with her back against her door, listening to her parents' voices from downstairs.

'In our culture, you respect your elders, you shameless child,' her parents shout at her.

Everyone keeps telling her about her culture this, her culture that. But it still makes no sense to her. Boys, sleepovers, make-up, shaving her stupid legs; none of this is part of her culture, or so her parents keep saying. But Abeer is not stupid; she knows culture is just an excuse.

She knows her culture, whatever it is, is meant to be richer than the absurd social restrictions placed on her life but at this moment in time she thinks this culture everyone else talks about, whatever it might be, is the culprit behind everything that is wrong with her life. So she begins to fight it in small ways which later will seem insignificant but are momentous right now because she is 15 and angry at all the ways she does not fit in.

She buys a short black skirt from a cheap closing-down store on her way home through town and hides it in her school bag. The next day, she wears the mini underneath her regulation-length skirt, her heart thumping all the while because she knows she is breaking all sorts of rules her mother has made her swear by. She runs to the toilets as soon as she gets to school and skims off her longer skirt to reveal the shorter one underneath. She cannot believe what she has done and she pulls at her skirt, smoothing it out above her knees.

'Nice skirt, A Beer,' one of the girls says.

'Thanks,' she mumbles, from underneath the thick strands of hair that still fall over the front of her face, her adrenaline blinding her to the intended sarcasm.

'Still a hairy Paki beast under the tights though,' another girl snorts, kicking at Abeer's legs, before they all laugh.

That lunch hour, Abeer locks herself in a toilet cubicle and hugs her knees, pulling at the threads in her tights with her nails until they pucker and split, revealing little patches of her bare skin. Her eyes tremble with tears which she tries to hold in but they roll down her face and sting the sides of her nose. She plucks at the hairs that she can see, trying desperately and impossibly to break them with her fingers but then ends up scratching her skin until it bleeds.

When the bell rings to sound the end of lunch, she takes out her regulation skirt, crumpled and creased, and puts it back on, feeling stupid and fat and hairy and ugly, all of those things at once.

After that day Abeer saves up her pocket money for a month, until she has enough to visit the salon in town one Saturday morning. She thinks she has waited long enough.

She makes an excuse, telling her parents she needs to select books for coursework from the library when, really, she is lying in a salon stripped down to her underwear and does not even register the pain as wax is poured onto her then torn from her skin, piece by piece.

It marvels her, the newfound soft skin on her arms and her legs and before she leaves the treatment room, she slathers on extra moisturising cream, which smells like breath mints and tingles her skin where the wax has been, before pulling up her jeans and rolling down her sleeves.

She feels dazzling, like a blinding full beam light, but later when she is clearing the plates from the dining table, her mother catches a glimpse of her smooth forearm, then takes her by the wrist and shoves up her sleeve and demands to know what she has done.

'Why? What can you do about it? It is done. It is too late,' Abeer laughs.

A decade from now when Abeer is 25, her mother will tell this story and laugh and shake her head at how much of a firecracker her daughter was, to go behind her back.

Abeer will laugh too but she will also flinch, because she still does not really understand why her mother was so against it and it embarrasses her to be reminded of what it was like to be 15. After the laughter subsides as this story is told, Abeer will fall quiet and softly say, 'You should have just let me do it sooner. You didn't handle it right. You know, right, that they teased me about it a lot at school?' Her mother will smile and wave Abeer away with her hand.

'You are so sensitive!' she will say. 'I did you a favour, making you wait that long. The younger you start all that waxing and shaving and plucking, the more of a headache it is.'

But later, when she is putting the dishes away, she will think to herself perhaps she should have been easier on Abeer. She will acknowledge that perhaps she did not always know how to bring her daughter up so far away from the way she herself had been raised. For a moment, she will rest the palms of her hands on the kitchen counter and she will consider how hurt her teenage daughter must have been by the names they called her at school, and she will ask herself why she did not realise it. She will ask herself why she had turned such silly things like clothes and make-up and waxing into such a great big deal when, really, it did not matter at all.

Years later, when Abeer is older, she will read a news article about a Sikh woman who refuses to touch her body hair because she believes her body is sacred.

Abeer will be mesmerised by the pictures and will marvel at this woman's faith and grace, knowing she could never be as strong. She will read comment pieces in newspapers which debate feminism and whether or not waxed and shaved legs have a place in it. She will read all of these pieces written by opinionated journalists and she will see their point and will think it is all very well and good, but she will wonder if they have any idea of what it might feel like to grow up being called a fat Paki hairy beast. She will wonder what they would have done about it if it had happened to them, when they were just 15.

She is 16. She is starting to learn to hate herself less.

She tops the year with her exam results and the triumph this brings lifts her up high. It buys her a small sum of independence in the form of gift money heaped inside congratulations cards from family friends who come to visit. They lavish praise on her parents, saying they have raised her so well, and though Abeer wants to point out that she was the one who did all the hard work and revised, she smiles because she knows what is inside the cards and cannot wait to count it all once their visitors have gone.

She uses her fortune, neat piles of ironed £10 and £20 notes, to book waxing appointments at the local salon and buy clothes to reinvent herself. Her mother is not altogether impressed by her shopping choices but she lets her spend her exam-result money as she likes because she knows by now it is a battle she will lose.

'What can I say? Even if I tell you no, you do not listen anyway,' her mother sighs.

Abeer does not care too much about her mother's exasperation. When she goes back to school in September, she will be a sixth-former and with that comes perks and a certain degree of freedom. She no longer has to take games lessons or do compulsory swimming and she no longer has to wear black skirts with thick black tights even in the summer to hide her legs.

Their year group will be split up, now that they will each be studying different subjects of their own choice with individual universities in mind, so she will not have to spend every day in a classroom with the shrieky girls who have spent all of her senior school years picking on her and calling her names. Abeer can start again. She cannot wait.

Abeer loves her afternoons shopping alone in town, a habit that will stay with her for years, but she does not delude herself. She is 16, and she knows she is not pretty like the other girls at school. She learns to choose clothes that hide the place where her thighs rub together and cover the bump around her stomach which she will never entirely ever lose. In the run-up to her waxing appointments at the salon, appointments which have become regular now since her first secret visit, she bristles at the feel of her follicles breaking through the surface of her skin and spoiling it all again and again.

But she knows now that the hair she hates so much will all come off, at least, and with the right clothes covering her, she might not be picked on as much. That is enough for now. It is okay, and okay is better than how she had felt before.

When Abeer returns to school at the end of this summer, she feels like she understands a little of what it is to be the sweet 16 her magazines talk about. She has new clothes and new eyebrows and no body hair. She wears her hair swept back with a wide headband because her upper lip is clean now and she looks different.

But when she enters the common room, she feels a heavy mass of anxiety creeping up behind her and poking over her shoulder and she worries that perhaps all this effort will backfire and that perhaps the pony-tailed girls will still find some way to break her again, to push her against the wall and make fun of her face.

But none of the others even notice she is there. They have too much of their own news, of summer romances and trips away, to even register that Abeer is also back. She is elated, because for the first time in all of her school years, she is left alone and nobody has called her a Paki beast. She whispers a small prayer of thanks and of hope that it might be over.

At the start of the new school term, Abeer wins a prize for her academic achievement and when she finds out that her name will be announced at assembly because of it, she takes her form tutor aside and asks if she can please pronounce it properly. Her teacher's pronunciation is not perfect and she stumbles slightly, but it is certainly better than A Beer.

When her name is said out loud, Abeer holds her breath. It takes a while for Abeer to realise the faint murmur she heard was one of girls quietly stunned because they had not considered her a contender for the prize.

They had not realised she was quite as clever as she was for she rarely answers questions in class.

For now, that does not matter to Abeer. Her name is not as hilariously ridiculous to the other girls at school as it was before and finally, Abeer feels as if she might have escaped the cruelty of the name-calling she put up with before. Her name was an old joke that lasted for years but finally, the other girls have simply moved on.

Her parents continue to phone all their relatives to let them know of her academic success. It embarrasses Abeer and annoys her too, because she feels as if they are taking the credit for the countless hours of revision she put in.

Besides Abeer thinks it is unfair because while they tell everyone else how well she has done, she does not hear it that much from them herself. They hugged her only perfunctorily, before starting to dial numbers and tell everyone else how she had done.

It will not be until much later that Abeer will realise they were not using her exam results to boast or show off, as she initially thought. When Abeer is a grown woman in her thirties, nearly twenty years from now, her mother will be washed out by cancer and she will take Abeer's hand and tell her all the things she never knew, like how when she came home with excellent exam results, the reason she did not hug her for too long was because she felt like she was about to cry and did not want to let her teenage daughter see her tears.

Even by then, Abeer will not know that while she is at work, busy in the litigation team of her city law firm, her mother will talk about her endlessly with the carers Abeer pays for, telling them how beautiful and how clever and how successful her daughter is.

When Abeer is older, she will return to her school every few years and each time she will be astonished by how many more young Pakistani girls she sees there, compared to the time when she was the only one. She will be invited back by headteachers, introduced as an example of the sort of woman the girls can grow to be, giving motivational speeches about her city career.

She will talk about what it is like in her workplace and when she does, she will always look for the quiet Asian girl who does not quite fit in, the one who sits on her own, looking sad and uncomfortable in her own skin, the one who thinks she is no one.

She will lock eyes with this girl, looking at her directly now and again during her speeches, willing her to know that it will be okay and that eventually this time, this awkward, horrible teen time that feels like the end of the world, will pass. She will look at this girl, the kind of girl she always was, who does not feel like she has a place to belong, and she will tell her silently not to worry, that she will make it anyway.

When Abeer is 35 and pregnant with her first child, she studies names with her husband. They consider easy names, names which sound English and will blend in, names like Adam and Sara, Zachariya and Leila. Abeer is determined to pick a name that will be effortless, a name that sounds normal. A name that could be from any place, anywhere. 'Not a name like Abeer,' she says only half-jokingly.

When her child is born, Abeer holds her in her arms and examines her dark crop of hair and her bright, shiny eyes with wonder. They toy with their list of preferred Anglicised names: Zara, Yasmin, Sophia.

Abeer tries calling her baby each of these names, one by one. But though they are beautiful names, she feels they are too vague.

While she traces the outline of her baby's nose, she calls her by a new name, one she had not considered before. 'Feroza,' she whispers. It is her late mother's name; a traditional Pakistani name.

She suggests it to her husband. 'So that she will know where she comes from,' she says with tears in her eyes. 'So that she will always know.'

When she holds her baby and she rocks her, she promises her she will learn from the mistakes her parents made. She promises her she will never let Feroza feel left out or alone or confused by the differences she sees in herself compared to others. It is a different time, now, and it is easier for Abeer to make these promises than it ever was for her parents. She does not blame them; they did not always know what to do. It was only when her mother first fell sick with cancer that she realised how hard it had been for them to find their way, how hard it was to raise a teenage daughter in a strange place. She had taken it all for granted, before.

She makes all these promises to her baby silently. But in promising so much, there will be new mistakes for Abeer to make. She has to make her own mistakes. She may not get everything right. But she has time. There is no rush.

6

English portions

Mrs Ajmal's dinner parties were legendary. Everyone talked about them.

'Have you been invited yet?' her friends asked each other over the phone.

'I don't know how she does it! So much work!' they all exclaimed.

Mrs Ajmal loved hosting her dinners. She did not complain about the preparation involved. She planned for them for weeks in advance, scribbling down menus and lists of elaborate dishes, most of which she knew off by heart but also new ones she had found in cookbooks or had invented entirely by herself.

She stuck her lists on the refrigerator door, pondering over her choices every time she opened it to take out milk for tea or butter for toast.

She studied her menus, examining the range of dishes and the variety of cuisines, adding question marks in biro here and there or swapping chicken for lamb, always thinking there was never enough for all of the guests she had called.

Sometimes she asked her husband for his suggestions while they both read in bed, propped up on their pillows. 'What do you think?' she said, her glasses perched on the edge of her nose, her spiral notepad in her hands. 'Mangalorean chicken or Kashmiri?' Her husband, reading the latest issue of the medical magazine he subscribed to, always replied in the same way,

'Whatever you make, my dear, it will be delicious,' he said. 'It always is.' Then, he leant over to kiss her goodnight, a brief and abrupt kiss on her lips but an affectionate one all the same.

Mrs Ajmal kept her most precious, most favourite cookbooks stacked on the bottom shelf of her bedside table. There were books her two boys had given to her on numerous birthdays, hefty tomes by Madhur Jaffrey and Julie Sahni, and a worn copy of Mrs Balbir Singh's *Indian Cookery* given to her by her mother-in-law when she left India to join her husband in England.

She thumbed, enchanted, through these books and the pages she knew by memory the way others lost themselves in romances or thrillers or the gossip pages of magazines. In Mrs Ajmal's mind each recipe was a plotline, slowly building up and then culminating in a magnificent crescendo, a final wondrous dish served upon a plate, tumbling from the pages of her books into tastes she could feel fizzing in her mouth like pops of lemonade, sometimes sour, sometimes sweet.

It was not always like this. When Mrs Ajmal first arrived in England in the 1970s as a young bride, she could not cook. Oh, but she loved food and she loved to eat. But she simply could not cook.

It was not her fault. She had not been expected to know her way around a kitchen. She grew up in a large, comfortable house with a cook called Ali to cater for the family's every meal and every craving, day and night.

Ali took care of everything. When her college friends came over late at night, he heated up bowls of gajar ka halwa for them, which they scooped up with teaspoons, scraping every last clump of sweet, syrupy carrot. On weekends, Ali always made her favourite snacks, chilli chicken legs and spiced salty chickpeas.

As a child, she was often running in and out of the kitchen to Ali, much to her mother's despair who thought she would be a hindrance there. But Ali never complained. He sat her up on the counter, offered her teaspoons of sweet milky kheer, unset and still warm from the pan, which she slurped like a kitten, greedy for more.

When her marriage was proposed, her mother-in-law suggested it might be a good idea for her to learn a few basic dishes before leaving for England, a simple chicken dish or biryani. But she never did. It did not occur to her to take the suggestion seriously.

'We will fill ourselves on love!' she said, teasingly, much to her mother and mother-in-law's horror. 'And when that is not enough, we shall dine out like royalty. We will think of something!'

When Mrs Ajmal first arrived in England she did not think she would miss India much. 'You could at least pretend to be sad,' said her sister on her wedding day and then again at the airport too, when the newly named Mrs Ajmal was about to leave for good. She was almost too enthusiastic to leave, a few relatives dryly observed.

But Mrs Ajmal was far too happy to be sad. She was not a tearful bride, but a smiling one, and one, her mother said, who talked far too much.

She had married a man, a cousin of her sister's husband, with whom she had shared a playful attraction since they had first met. It had gone on for months, a teasing, chaste flirtation performed cleverly away from their elders' eyes. It took the form of candid compliments and innocent gazes that lingered longer than necessary, mostly, Mrs Ajmal pointed out whenever her sister chided her, from his side not hers.

Whenever Mrs Ajmal went to visit her sister, the cousin always happened to casually appear. He had passed his medical exams and was soon to leave for England, and it was when he asked if he could write to Mrs Ajmal that her sister intervened. 'No. You should know better,' she scolded the cousin, taking him aside and directing him to speak to her father as soon as possible and not risk her sister's reputation.

It was a happy union. As a young couple who had courted each other playfully yet respectfully, without their fingertips so much as brushing before their wedding night, they were besotted with each other.

As they boarded the plane together, sharing a nervous sense of excitement, their romance grew. In England, they shared a newfound freedom to learn about each other and fall steadily into a love more lasting than their first, heady attraction, away from the watchful glare of both of their families. And so Mrs Ajmal did not miss her family, and she assuredly told them so every few weeks.

'What is there to miss?' she laughed loudly during the trunk calls her husband booked for her every fortnight. 'I have a husband! We are too much in love!'

But although she would not admit that she missed her family, of course she did, deep down. Her husband had warned her that it would not necessarily be easy at first so early on in his career. Though he was a doctor it would still take years, he said, before they could afford their own home. And it might be yet more years, he added, before they could buy airline tickets to visit their families again. Mrs Ajmal said she did not mind about all that. She was simply happy to be with him.

But, still, it was quiet in their small, rented flat in Oxford which had been provided for them by the hospital where her husband worked. He was often on call and worked long nights, and during those nights there was silence and a stillness that Mrs Ajmal had never heard before.

In the house in Delhi where she grew up, there were always doors slamming, people shouting, visitors shuffling forever in and out of her daily life.

Cousins and family friends arrived unannounced and uninvited at odd hours but were still welcomed in, sipping masala chai from stainless steel cups. In Hindi, there was a word for it, for the noise and the chatter and the liveliness of it all.

'I miss the raunak,' she said sadly to her husband one night, when he came home exhausted from a hospital shift and she flung her arms around him.

There was something else missing too. Mrs Ajmal was always hungry. Most days she met her husband in the hospital canteen for lunch or an early breakfast if he had worked through the night, but she could not feel excited about bland things like cold toast and baked beans or dry potatoes which were stuffed with a flavourless bright yellow cheese. The sloppy food served up in the hospital canteen reminded her every day of how sickeningly hungry she was for the flavours of home and for the people she shared that food with too.

Early on in their marriage, her husband surprised her with a table for two reserved at an Indian restaurant nearby. Mrs Ajmal dressed in a midnight blue sari, radiant and ravenous.

But the food was not what she was used to; the korma too pale and sweet, the mince too shrivelled. She tried to look pleased, but her husband knew himself that it was not the sort of Indian food that either of them was used to.

Some days, when she was so hungry it hurt and another blanched canteen vegetable lodged in her throat, Mrs Ajmal thought that out of everyone in Delhi, she missed Ali the cook most of all.

Her husband had told her, before their marriage, of how beautiful a city Oxford was. She could not deny its beauty, its regal charm, but she also found it haughty, cold. She longed to warm her hands with hot samosas, crumbling potato and peas wrapped in thick, fat pastry. She craved pani puri, crispy fried globes which she would pop with her thumb and stuff with sour tamarind sauce and swollen chickpeas and sharp onions that stung her tongue, the same snacks she used to buy with her friends from the street vendors outside their college gates. She missed the taste of home, the smell of it, the sound of it, the stain of it on her hands.

Mrs Ajmal was astonished and only slightly ashamed to learn her husband knew more about cooking than she did. When he came back early from his hospital shifts, he boiled rice and simmered dhaal, sometimes yellow, sometimes green, which they ate together from bowls.

Sometimes, he gently encouraged her, phoning her from the doctors' mess to remind her to soak the lentils before he came home, later asking her to take over the stirring of the pan while he took a bath or to fry some diced onion and garlic until crispy enough to scatter on top.

He tried not to make her feel bad, telling her that he had not expected her to know how to do it all herself, given her privileged upbringing. 'But it is enjoyable, turning ingredients into a simple meal,' he said, gesturing towards the small bags of dry rice and pulses and spices which he kept on the kitchen counter, the open packets stuck down with sticky tape to keep them fresh. 'There is a sense of achievement in it. You should give it a go.'

Each mouthful she shared with her husband reminded Mrs Ajmal of the flavours she missed, and so one day she pulled out the cookbook her mother-in-law had packed her off with, and slowly began to try, nervously slicing onions and crushing cloves of garlic with the palm of her hand positioned over the cool blade of a knife.

She pinched open the leathery skins of cardamom shells, popping out little black seeds which she crushed into an uneven powder with a rolling pin. She grated knobbly chunks of ginger until the tips of her fingers bled and stirred puddles of spices the colours of the leaves of Oxford trees in autumn, staining her good saris with flecks of watery turmeric that splashed up at her and made her jump back from the stove in surprise.

At the beginning, it was disastrous. Her boneless chicken too dry, her lamb chops too tough, her chopped onions burnt and black at the bottom of the saucepan, coated in a bitter paste of overcooked dry spices. 'It's just practice, that's all,' her husband said, rubbing her back whenever she felt like giving up.

But then, slowly, she started to have more success. It took months, but eventually her biryani spooned out in tumbling layers of rice and chunks of meat, threads of saffron laced delicately throughout. Her kebabs no longer crumbled like soft clay but held together, shaped like the chubby thumbs of a toddler. 'Excellent,' her husband declared, at the end of each meal.

In one of her fortnightly long-distance calls to her mother, she asked for Ali's recipes. Her mother replied, bemused, 'Ali does not follow "recipes". It is all in his head!' But Mrs Ajmal insisted, asking her mother to transcribe Ali's directions for her while he cooked.

The recipes took an eternity to arrive, thin papers covered in her mother's handwriting bundled together in large packets covered with stamps. She sifted through the sheets, making lists of the ingredients she would need. Her husband drove her as far as Luton or Leicester where they had been told the best-stocked Indian food shops were. They returned at the end of the day, their car stuffed with bags of spices and gram flour, tins of chickpeas and tubs of clarified butter.

Later, when Mrs Ajmal fell pregnant for the first time, she craved fresh, warm naans like Ali used to make. She leafed through the papers her mother had sent, found the recipe and surprised herself by making them on her own, mounding and shaping heaps of wet, sticky flour with her hands, impatiently waiting for the dough to rise.

She watched as her naans puffed up quickly in the oven like magic, then dripped ghee generously all over them. She ate them all, much to her husband's amusement, leaning casually with her back against the kitchen counter, one hand resting on her stomach, the other tearing each naan one by one into small, pillowy pieces which she savoured, ever so satisfied.

After that pregnancy and the next, she never quite lost the soft roundness she gained, but it did not upset her. She loved to cook and she loved to eat and it suited her, the extra plumpness that cushioned her cheeks and cradled her chin and peeped through her sari.

'I am as round as a kofta!' she laughed with her husband, her hands covering her belly. 'I am as stuffed as a paratha!'

Mrs Ajmal's passion for cooking took over her days. She scribbled her own adaptations on Ali's recipes which her mother had sent her, and began to look at her mother-in-law's cookbook less and less, becoming more adventurous in experimenting with flavours on her own. She no longer needed to check if her masala required one teaspoon of cumin or two; she could sense it by the smell alone.

She cooked in abundance, more than they needed at home and sent her husband to work with finger food he could share with his colleagues, something different every week; aloo tikki, samosas, Indian spring rolls. He brought back empty plastic containers, compliments from his colleagues who asked for more.

Once, when Mrs Ajmal was still a newlywed and had only recently discovered her flair for cooking, she accompanied her husband to a sit-down dinner at the home of one of his English colleagues. The table was set neatly for three sets of couples, soft music in the background low enough so they could converse over candlelight.

Mrs Ajmal smiled at her hosts and the other guests, while inside she marvelled at the formality of it all. This was not the raunak she had hoped for.

The food, too, was not as generous as she had hoped. Individual plates were warmed in the oven. Starters and mains were brought out plate by plate, pre-portioned by the hosts. Dessert came later, a dark chocolate soufflé in a tiny glass dish that looked like it was part of a child's playset.

Mrs Ajmal finished it in two spoonfuls. Time went slowly, the conversation almost too polite to flow spontaneously. She was disappointed but also amused.

In the car on the way home, Mrs Ajmal laughed out loud. 'These Angrez loag! They just don't know how to serve! These English portions! Not even offers of seconds! Darling, I'm starving!'

Her husband patted her knee, indulging her with a few laughs of his own. He did not mean to be unappreciative of his colleague and his wife's hospitality, but he also agreed. It was not that the food was cooked badly, but that there was simply so little of it to eat in comparison to the plates his wife produced at home.

'No one can cook like us,' his wife said.

'No dear,' he corrected her. 'No one can cook quite like *you*.'

Mrs Ajmal laughed some more and then turned, twisting her seat belt, to face her husband.

'I could do better than that,' she said. 'Let's throw a party of our own.'

Mrs Ajmal's dinner parties were small to start off with. They invited the few Indian people that they knew, a group of hospital doctors who had only recently arrived in England. Some were bachelors, settled in temporary accommodation or shared houses, some were married and came with their wives, women Mrs Ajmal had not yet met before. Others were waiting for their wives to arrive, and the married men teased these ones, saying their freedom was about to end. It was a time before any children had been born, the married couples still all newlyweds, still all treasuring the freedom they had with their spouses away from their families overseas.

Some of the wives were shy and uncertain about each other. At first, they exchanged pleasantries, asking where each was from, what they had studied, how long they had been married, what their rented accommodation was like.

But as Mrs Ajmal heaped mounds of rice and peas onto platters and ladled mutton curry and chunks of chicken floating in golden gravy from steel pots into Pyrex dishes, their quiet reservations quickly fell away.

There were no formalities here. Mrs Ajmal's guests sat casually wherever there was room, on the sofa, the few dining-table chairs or squashed on the large embroidered cushions she kept on the floor. They ate the food Mrs Ajmal had made, plentiful amounts, helping themselves without hesitation to more and more. They felt at ease with every plateful, as if they had known each other for years.

Suddenly it was the middle of the night, so much later than they had anticipated their evening would end, and although she felt tired as they ushered the last guests out quietly so as not to disturb other doctors in the neighbouring hospital flats, Mrs Ajmal felt content, like she had found her raunak again at last.

Mrs Ajmal's dinners became a regular event, taking place at least once a month, establishing her reputation among their small circle of friends as a fantastic cook. 'It's nothing,' she said, when her appreciative guests complimented her yet again on a feast.

Mrs Ajmal thought there was nothing complicated or fancy about what she had prepared. She simply made the food she had always loved to eat, the food that reminded her of home. Yet in her mind what she made was never quite as good as the memory of the meals Ali had once prepared.

She always cooked the dishes she knew her guests loved as much as she did, unfussy meaty salaans, vegetables cooked in heaps of fresh ginger and garlic, fiery, dry karhis served with bundles of naans. Her mother and her sister did not quite believe her when she told them, over the phone, what she had made. But she also began to experiment too, trying out different recipes from books she sought out at the library, things she had never had before, macaroni and bolognaise, throwing in dried hot peppers to liven them up.

The other couples began to extend invitations for dinners to their homes too, all of them teasing the bachelors about the hundreds of meals they owed in debt. And so the moments of loneliness that Mrs Ajmal initially endured trickled away, absorbed into an almost never-ending circle of lunches and dinners and last-minute calls to come over for tea.

'There's so much raunak here!' Mrs Ajmal told her sister and her mother during their long-distance phone calls.

It was in this way that Mrs Ajmal and her husband formed friendships that would last forever. Though they were brought together largely by chance and professions, they shared so much, all of these young husbands and wives and bachelors who had come from India or sometimes Pakistan.

They had all arrived in England young and determined and hopeful, all of them far away from their families and their homes. They were unrooted and unsettled by choice in a place where they hoped they might achieve more than they could have had they stayed in the country where they were born.

They strived. Husbands worked long hours, dedicated to their medical professions. Wives budgeted carefully, planning monthly household expenditure on limited salaries. But they also enjoyed themselves.

In the beginning, it was an experience for them. On weekends they shared cars and took day trips to cities like London and Bath where they loaded their cameras with film and snapped themselves in front of famous monuments, pictures the women would later paste into large photo albums or send tucked inside thin, folded letters to their families.

The wives cut their hair into short bobs and swapped saris and shalwar kameez for smocks and flares while the husbands began buying English broadsheets and discussing the prime minister and political parties with the same fervour as they did Partition.

But though they had made some English friends, mostly their neighbours who were also hospital staff, the English ways did not always make sense to them.

The wives tried but they all agreed it was hard to make friends with other English women. They smiled at shop assistants and tried to chat to receptionists and the women who served them at the bank, but their encounters were always perfunctory and hardly conducive to friendship.

And so it was easier, they all thought, to seek out familiar coloured skins and familiar flavoured food and speak to each other in their mother tongue. They forged a connection, extending helping hands whenever they heard a new doctor had arrived from India or Pakistan in town, lending things that were too big and impractical to bring with them from overseas, like extra bedding or winter coats. Some doctors, mostly the bachelors who were more open to job postings elsewhere, left and moved on. But they always took care to swap addresses, posting letters and birthday cards.

Those that stayed in the same area became even closer. With time, they watched each other's families grow, becoming aunts and uncles to children who would never know their faraway blood relatives the way they would their parents' friends.

Their children played with each other like cousins. They became family. They hardly missed India or Pakistan any more for they had made their own version of it for themselves, here, inside each other's homes.

After they had been married for five years, Mrs Ajmal's husband calculated that they could afford to buy their own home on a quiet, residential road and finally move out of the latest of the numerous small rented flats they had lived in.

Mrs Ajmal longed for a large kitchen of her own. The house they bought was modest, but the rooms were ample in size. Attached to the kitchen was a small pantry, where Mrs Ajmal stored tins and dried food and heavy pans, and her husband put up shelves where she could rest her growing collection of cookery books.

A few days after they had unpacked and settled in, Mrs Ajmal introduced herself to their English neighbours. She knocked on doors, distributing trays of samosas and chutneys, the spice levels carefully tempered, while her two little boys clasped bowls of sweet, milky *rasmalai* between their hands, holding them out carefully in front as their mother had ordered.

One by one her neighbours knocked on her door, returning empty bowls. 'Delicious, Mrs Ajmal! What was in that chutney? And that sweet pudding! You must show me how to make it!' they said.

And so with time, her food formed surprising new friendships. Food became a way for her to make bonds with well-heeled English women she assumed for so long she had little in common with.

She swapped recipes with women down the road and across it, learned to make food she had never considered before. With their help, she created mountainous pavlovas topped with berries and snowy whipped cream, presented her husband and her sons with Sunday roasts and vol-au-vents filled with mushrooms and cheese.

Her new friends introduced her to baking, lending her cake tins and whisks, much to her sons' delight. And in turn, she taught them spicy marinades to rub on legs of lamb and simple chicken dishes, showing them easy little tricks like how to cook white rice perfectly, steaming it in the oven once the water was drained.

She prepared packets of fresh spices for them, including whole cloves, cardamom pods and cinnamon sticks, urging them to throw away the bottles of ready-made curry powders they bought from the supermarket, which, she explained, did not taste authentic at all.

Later, when her boys were both in primary school, she sent them into school with large tupperware boxes stacked with little rounds of nankhati which she had baked instead of cakes for their stall at their school Christmas fair. Her eldest son fussed at first, asking her if she could make something else, embarrassed because he knew all the other mothers had made Victoria sponges layered with jam and walnut loaves. But her crumbly, buttery biscuits disappeared before any of the other treats, people licking the tips of their fingers to pick up crumbs of crushed pistachio as fine as sand which had fallen onto their clothes, asking her sons to tell their mother to make more. From that point onwards, Mrs Ajmal began to make them every year, presenting teachers and the parents of her sons' school friends with boxes of Indian biscuits, tied with ribbon. It became her own Christmas tradition.

Over the years, Mrs Ajmal's dinner parties became noisier, bigger affairs, with a headcount of fifty people, at the very least, packed into her home.

When she first started her parties, there were perhaps only ten or eleven guests. But their social circle quickly spiralled, couples introducing yet more new arrivals to the area from overseas, and by now they all had families too. While some of their oldest friends lived just minutes away, as they had all long since left hospital accommodation and had recommended the same neighbourhood to each other to live in long term, others drove an hour each way to join them from different towns.

Little children played precariously on the stairs, eating soft rice and raita from coloured paper bowls with plastic spoons which Mrs Ajmal kept especially for them. Mrs Ajmal's teenage boys took the older children upstairs where they sat huddled together on the floor, eating in front of the television in the guest room and watching films or playing computer games, with strict orders not to spill their fizzy drinks.

There were so many guests, they sat divided among different rooms, the men in one, the women in another. It was harder to fit everyone into the dining room at the same time, so they took it in shifts, her sons passing out plates to their guests and keeping an eye on which dishes needed to be refilled. The men always went first, then the children, then the wives.

It went on like this for decades. There were parties celebrating every milestone, a birthday, a promotion or their boys securing places at university. On their parents' twentieth anniversary, Mrs Ajmal's sons suggested their mother take a rest.

'Why don't you and Abu go out for dinner for a change, instead of you cooking again?' they said. But she would not listen.

'Where is the fun in that?' she asked.

And so she picked up the phone and called all of her friends, inviting eighty people around for dinner instead.

But as soon as her sons went to university, they started to complain about the parties their mother threw on the weekends they returned home to visit. 'It's boring,' they said. 'There's too many people. It's tiring. We just want to come home and relax instead, or catch up with our own friends.'

And so her parties slowly started to diminish. At first she enjoyed the free time. She had never counted the hours taken up with the food shopping, the chopping, the preparation of it all. But even though it gave her more time to spend with her husband, allowing them time to watch films and take walks together, it still saddened her deeply.

She still received many invites to other dinners at other people's homes, but she missed the raunak and the noise in her own home, even more so now that her sons lived away at different universities. 'It makes no sense,' she said sadly to her husband. 'They say they want to relax at home, tell me not to invite people over, and yet they go out with their friends anyway. Even when they come to visit, they are never here.'

Mrs Ajmal felt her sons, with their ready-made social lives and their confident ease, did not understand that her dinners had meant more to her than merely socialising.

In the beginning, Mrs Ajmal's parties filled a void. They created noise, the clatter of plates and clamour of voices talking all at the same time, which stifled the stillness she first encountered in the early days. Her dinners brought strangers together who all came from the same place and had made the same journey to start new lives. They shared the food that reminded them all of home and quickly, they were not strangers any more.

But as her sons grew older, she realised she did not want them to miss out on this, on the Indian sense of spirit, the raunak that she so loved.

Mrs Ajmal knew she could not give her sons cousins living in the house next door or grandparents who could pick them up from school, for continents divided them too far. But she could give them a sense of it, she thought, through the friends she had made with her husband all those years ago, who had been a part of their life ever since that first dinner in their small, rented flat. She recreated a little Indian world for her sons in their detached Oxford home. Except now, as her sons have grown older, it feels as if they no longer want to be a part of it.

Her husband puts his arms around her from time to time and tells her not to take it so personally, that the boys have simply grown up. But Mrs Ajmal feels as if it is more than that.

There is no one for Mrs Ajmal to pass along the flavours of her favourite foods to. Her sons have never been interested in cooking, and her daughter-in-laws prefer making quick pasta dishes after work or trying out recipes from the celebrity chefs they have seen on television when they have the time. No one wants to sift through Mrs Ajmal's folder which holds Ali's recipes written in her dead mother's neat hand, her own adjustments scribbled on the side.

Now Mrs Ajmal is approaching her seventieth birthday. She started making lists of dishes to cook, of friends she wanted to invite. But her sons and their wives have convinced her not to invite each and every one of her friends for dinner again. They have booked a table at an upmarket Iranian restaurant for them to celebrate together. 'It will be just us,' they say. 'Just the family. You will enjoy it. You deserve a break. And you will love the food, you'll see.'

At the restaurant, the family sits around a large table. The music is soft and low, and the lights are dim. Her grandchildren long to sit on her lap, but their parents tell them to sit still and behave. She sits next to her husband, opposite her sons. Her sons order for her, and her daughter-in-laws present her with gifts and kisses on her cheek. There are no cookbooks this year, there have not been for years, but there are expensive perfumes in gift bags and Mrs Ajmal smiles. Her husband reaches for her hand, and she smiles some more, but inside she marvels at the formality of it all and wonders where all the raunak has gone.

7

Potluck

It is long past midnight when Ladli quietly clicks the corded phone which hangs unsteadily on the wall back into its cradle. She stands and places her hands in the nook of her lower back and arches luxuriously upwards like the inquisitive curves of her eyebrows and allows herself for a moment to imagine Sunil's hands there instead.

She would be in so much trouble, if everyone knew.

Ladli has spent over an hour sitting on the low stool in the kitchen in the dark, while her sister and her mother sleep, whispering excitedly to Sunil. She bites her lower lip and suppresses her smile.

Ladli is not ready to sleep, even though she promised Sunil she would go to bed and dream of him. He has left her wide awake and she is humming with her secrets of him and of them and of what tomorrow, when they will slip away together from college for the day, will bring.

She reaches up and twists her oiled hair at the nape of her neck, feeling tiny dots of damp sweat pop through her skin and settle into the old, mismatched shalwar kameez she wears for sleeping in. Tomorrow morning before college, she will wash away the oil her sister rubbed roughly into her scalp which makes her hair feel even heavier in this heat and she will feel fresh again, the way Sunil only ever knows her to be.

Ladli is glad that Sunil has never seen her like this, in her tattered and stale summer night-clothes and she wishes, not for the first time, that they had air conditioning like the bigger houses in the newer compounds where all the richer people lived.

Ladli hears the back gate click open and fall closed. Her father is finally home. She squints at her wristwatch in the dim light and wonders how much he lost tonight. She wonders, quickly, whether to ask him as she hears him approach the back door. But instead, Ladli slips behind the thin curtain which hangs in front of what they call the store, an alcove lined with shelves supporting bags and buckets of dry food and bottles of their mother's sweet and sour pickles, and she waits for him to pass.

When she hears him disappear behind the door of the room he shares with her mother, Ladli comes out from behind the curtain and with the stealth of a jewellery thief she tiptoes her way to the room where she sleeps side by side with her older sister Suki on a thin mattress laid out on the floor.

She is relieved she did not speak to her father tonight. He might have asked her why she is still awake. Besides, she will know soon enough by her mother's tears just how much her father lost tonight. She slips under the flimsy sheet covering her mattress, and begins to dream of Sunil as she falls asleep.

The morning is chaotic. Suki is running late for work because Ladli is taking too long in the bath, leisurely washing away the oil in her hair with more shampoo than she needs. Suki shouts at her sister to hurry while thumping on the bathroom door. Ladli slips out in a towel and grins but Suki gives her a scowling shove out of the way and tells her to cover up, calling her shameless, behsharam.

Their father is not yet awake, so Suki will take the bus and then the train alone today to the jewellery shop, where they normally work side by side mending broken beaded necklaces, rethreading semi-precious strings of glittering gems and resizing rich women's thick, gold rings for fingers which seem to get plumper every day.

'Another day doing all that work on my own,' grumbles Suki, returning to the bedroom to quickly get changed.

'Cheer up,' says Ladli, stretching her eyelid with one hand and painting a thick black pointed line along it with the other. 'You're supposed to be the happy bride,' she says, blinking with wide, peering eyes in the mirror at the clumps of mascara coating her lashes. Suki looks at her, unimpressed.

Their mother is already in the kitchen, going through the orders she has collected from neighbours and the small local grocery shops which stock her jars of pickle. When Ladli comes downstairs, she is standing in front of the store, counting and calculating how many more bottles she needs to make today. She looks so small, all curved in on herself, like one of the tiny, perfectly formed seashells Suki used to collect when they were little girls to make bracelets with.

There is already tea on the stove and slices of thin chilli omelette their mother has prepared, lacy with oil and cut into quarters long gone cold on a plate for Ladli and Suki to share. Their father's portion is set aside for when he will awake.

Her mother turns around to face Ladli, holding her notepad with her pickle orders written in pencil in her hand. Her small, bony face is set almost permanently in a worried expression, as if the wind once blew on her while she forced her thin eyebrows together to form a straight-lined frown, thinking and serious, and made her stay that way forever.

'Your Papa-ji,' she begins. 'He is not well. Tell Suki to hurry because she cannot be late today. Not if she is working alone.'

Ladli swallows a papery piece of lightly greased omelette, onions stinging her throat.

'How much?' she asks, ignoring her mother's request for her to call her sister and instead leaning back in her chair, legs outstretched like a teenager ready to sulk though she is past those years, even if only just. 'Last night, how much did he lose this time?'

Her mother looks at her, stern and sharp for a moment, but then she pauses and loosens her jaw, too tired to scold. 'More than we can afford,' she says with quiet, softly lined sadness.

For a second, Ladli's mother stands still as if she wants to say something more. But then quickly she moves back into her pragmatic position in front of the store, furrowed once more over her notepad, costing and calculating out loud how many bottles of her homemade pickles she needs to sell this week.

Ladli picks at her cold, oiled omelette. She cannot wait for Sunil to take her away from all this. She cares for them, her Ma perhaps more than her Papa-ji, but she is tired and she is bored of the unspoken debt suspended over them, swinging slowly and heavily like the building cranes that hang precariously over the bigger, newer, richer housing compounds she passes every day on the way to college. Sunil says they might be able to afford an apartment there in a few years, shiny and clean with parking and air conditioning, once he starts work full-time and has a chance to save.

But for now, Ladli must live with her parents, where she feels like she is always told that she cannot buy this and she cannot go there. She must wait for Sunil but she cannot do anything until Suki goes first.

Ladli wishes Suki would hurry up, or at least insist on a wedding date after all this time. Suki has been engaged for two years now, but the wedding keeps getting delayed. The first year, it was the groom's side who postponed the wedding out of respect and grief when a grandmother died. The second year, it was Suki herself, who wanted to finish a jewellery design course she had saved for herself.

Then, finally, the wedding was arranged to take place two months ago, but this time, it was her father who hesitated.

'These girls, they take so long to decide. Which sari, which shoes, which jewellery,' he joked, when he went to visit his future son-in-law's family to ask if they could postpone again. The groom's side like Suki and her fiancé and her in-laws have been patient enough to wait, but Ladli and Suki's Papa-ji did not tell the truth when he went to visit the groom's side that day. He has not told them that, really, Suki did not care for fickle wedding finery but that even if she did, he had not the means to fund it.

It was his neighbour who introduced him to it, during one of their late-night smokes over the back gates. He confided he had no savings at all and certainly not enough for the expected dowry of one daughter, let alone two.

Their dowries had bothered him ever since they became teenagers, when his wife started buying shawls, weightless like the paper wings of dead moths, and bright saris folded inside cheap plastic covers. She started stowing them away carefully in suitcases under their bed, one for each child. When Suki got engaged, he could not keep hiding from the expectations her dowry was supposed to bring. He needed to do something.

There was never quite enough money to run the house. He did not know where it went for there never seemed to be just one, big expense. Instead, there were lots of things, endless things. Bills, house repairs, food. There was never anything left. Money just vanished, slowly dissolving like the thin, grey threads of cigarette smoke he exhaled sleeplessly at night, until there was nothing left but a stubby end, a few scraps of cash each month.

Even when Suki started working alongside him at the jewellers, it made little difference. Later, he hoped her completion of the design course might have helped, but her pay did not increase. Money came, and then it went.

At first, he started small. It was just a few rupees on a few card games with his neighbour and a few other men he did not know, collected from here and there. They watched cricket, smoked and secretly ate meat dishes their devout wives never cooked for them at home. They sat inside dark back rooms of ramshackle restaurants, throwing dice and tossing down cards and passing worn, crumpled rupee notes between their rough hands at the end of the night.

These nights offered him respite from home life, where his wife talked of Suki's wedding to come without realising the costs that he charted in his head. He did not tell her where he was; he could not. He made vague excuses for being late or for not being home and she accepted his little white lies like unassuming flowers.

'If this works,' he thought to himself at every game, marvelling at his small gains, 'if this works, I'll be able to pay for it all.'

He played well. He pocketed well. He was good around the card table and he did not want to stop. To his surprise, he realised when he thumbed the extra notes he had collected in his wallet that he had won far more than he had thought and he felt magnificent. He was not just the man who sat in the back, crouched over a lamp fixing fanciful jewellery other men could afford to buy for their wives.

But the nights got longer. The stacks of notes they played for got thicker. The mood was no longer that of men escaping from their homes and their wives for a while, but that of bitterness and rivalry. As a newcomer at the table he had done well, but the existing players did not like it. They demanded their money back, they demanded he play it all.

Under pressure his hands trembled and round after round he began to lose, uncomprehending and cheated by his hand, his money fading once more like cigarette smoke teasing in the air while some of the others sneered. He could not leave; they would not let him. Even now, he still plays every week, hoping for just one more win which he tells himself will make things better.

It was Suki who realised. She spent every day with her father, next to him at work, and she knew. She noticed the changes, the worry showing itself in the way he stared into space or chose to sit by himself. She noticed his agitation, his trembling hands. She noticed the irrational outbursts when he accidentally dropped a pearl or a bead or let a metal clasp slip, little things ordinarily but which her father somehow managed to turn into monumental mistakes, unleashing fury at himself.

She noticed the stacks of bills he hid in his desk drawer at work, rather than risk leaving at home, and she noticed all the late payments and last requests. It was Suki, who locked the door to the jewellery shop after they had finished work one night, and made him sit in front of her and explain everything.

Later too, it was Suki who spoke to her mother and to Ladli, whom she had called to sit with her on the sofa, while their father crouched in the corner with his head in his hands, broken and ashamed. There were problems, she said, about money, 'paisa ki baat.'

She said they all had to help in some way, her eyes pointedly fixed on Ladli, her spoilt little sister who had never considered money before. Suki started going through piles of bills, paying them off one by one, putting cash whenever she could into envelopes she labelled food, gas, electricity and Ladli.

Secretly, Ladli thinks her father is stupid. She does not understand why, after Suki sat them down on the sofa, they must still pretend like he has given up his late-night card games and his losing habit when they know he has not. She does not understand why Suki made her give up things like her mobile phone or buying the latest fashions or going to the cinema, when it is not Ladli's fault that they have lost everything.

She watches her mother, who must now spend another hot day in front of the gas stove making pickles for pittance so they can buy food to eat, and she rolls her eyes in frustration at her father, who sleeps while the rest of them must carry on.

She is making this face, sullen and fed-up, in silence as Suki bounds into the kitchen rushing to make it out of the back door. 'Suki! Breakfast, at least?' cries her mother, but it is too late.

Suki's jewellery kit bag, weighed down by her pouches of tools and packets of countless semi-precious beads and shells she crafts with, making her own things whenever the shop is quiet, is slung across her and she is already slipping into her sandals and shaking her head.

'No time, Ma,' she says. 'I can't be late. I will miss the bus, and if I miss the bus, I will miss the train and if I miss the train, well ...' Suki glances at Ladli gravely which suddenly makes Ladli think she might know about her plans to skip college and see Sunil today.

'Be good,' Suki says.

'I'm not 5!' says Ladli, pouting by way of reply.

Ladli waits for Sunil halfway down the street on the third right after the college gates, in front of the house with the dull blue metal gates. Serious couples like them do not meet at the bookshop or the coffee shop or the park where all the usual flirts and daters gather.

Ladli can just about see the other college couples, the ones with no shame who are not serious about each other, and she snorts, shaking her head, as she spies girls from her class tossing their hair and giggling with scruffy boys from Sunil's year who hand out compliments like chewing gum.

She feels sorry for these girls. They do not know these boys are not serious about them, not the way Sunil is about her. She feels superior, with her steady boyfriend and love marriage all planned out, even though it is all still a secret.

As she watches the girls down the street, she hears the nasal beep of the motorbike Sunil rides and he slows down to a stop and cocks his head to one side, motioning to her to jump on.

'Looks like you got your beauty sleep,' he says.

'I was dreaming of you,' she murmurs into his back.

Suki is a few streets away from Ladli's college, waiting for the bus. She dislikes taking the bus to the railway station when her father is not with her. It is not because he proves to be good commuting company, but because at least when it is clear her father is near her, the men on the bus do not look her up and down with dead eyes of dull lust, staring so obviously at her chest or her behind. Or at least, they do not do it so much.

She hates the hot murmurs of so-called approval she hears behind her, muttered low but just loud enough for her to hear. She hates it when yet another male passenger boards and passes closer than necessary, skimming her as she stands holding the rail where she can, a desperate sweaty hand slipping to touch the small of her back through her shirt or, sometimes, the clasp of her bra.

She hates the bus and she hates being late for work and she hates arriving on her own. She will have to explain to Mr Devi that her father is not coming in today, again. She will have to work twice as hard to make up for it.

She wishes she could move on from simply fixing jewellery; she has designs she sketches in her notebook that she would love to be able to make. It is strange, because Suki has never cared for girlish things like make-up and clothes like Ladli, but it is jewellery that takes her breath away.

Ever since she was a girl and threaded seashells collected from the beach into bracelets for her little sister, she has loved the intricacy of making something beautiful, even if it is mostly for someone else. She thinks of this, of the thin bracelets and the small, exquisite earrings and the jewellery she is making slowly for her own wedding day sketched in her pad, as she grits her teeth and fixes her jaw in frustration, staring straight ahead of her and waiting for her bus journey to end.

Ladli and Sunil are caught in traffic in front of the railway station as they weave their way to one of their favourite shopping malls. Once there, they will drink milkshakes under air conditioning and they will walk hand-in-hand and window shop, Sunil pointing out all the things he would buy her if he could, and later they will watch a matinee in the cinema, she does not mind which film, and she will let Sunil's hands find her in the dark.

Ladli thinks of this as she rests her head on Sunil's damp shirt and wraps her arms around him tighter. He briefly pats her hand, but then he raises his voice and swears at the bus packed with morning commuters jumping off on their way to work which has pulled out in front of him without the driver even checking he was there.

Suki fights her way to the front of the bus; she will miss the train to the city if she does not hurry. She jumps off without looking, swinging her jewellery kit bag, and does not notice the boy on the motorbike creeping up on the inside lane. She is startled by the horn and stutters backwards for a split second, waving her hand by way of apology to the motorbike rider when she notices the girl, peering over his shoulder.

Their eyes click into place like magnets. She sees Ladli, with her hair loose and her arms wrapped around a boy, and stops. 'Behanji, sister, move, yaar, for God's sake,' says the boy, gesturing and revving at her so that she steps off the road.

Suki is so surprised she does not even think to call her sister's name and simply says 'Oh.' But they have both seen each other. She raises her hand once more and runs across the road, and then she stands for a moment watching the bike disappear.

She shakes her head to snap out of her incredulity. It is too late to worry about Ladli right now. She turns, and breaks into a run, her sandals scuffing against the ground, to make it to the platform in time.

Ladli feels sick on the back of Sunil's bike. She should have known Suki could have been on any one of the buses heading in that direction of town. She feels hot and then cold and she loosens her grip on Sunil's waist. She is glad Sunil cannot see her face.

But Suki has seen her, her secret is out now. She feels sick and she cannot think straight and although she tells herself to calm down, that there will be some excuse or the other she can make, she knows that, really, she has been caught out. They are close to the mall and there is nothing she can do about it, not now.

The train is at the platform, to Suki's relief, and she scans it quickly, up and down, for the women's carriage which she always prefers when her father is not around. No pinching, no comments, more chance of a seat. But it is packed already, women hanging out the door. 'Jaldi, jaldi,' shouts one at her direction. 'Hurry! The train is leaving!'

Suki, who is still thinking of Ladli on the back of the motorbike with a boy, runs to jump on, but her bag gets in the way. She fumbles with the strap as she reaches up and grabs a rail with one hand, but her sandal slips and now the train is moving, first inching then rapidly picking up pace. Her foot drops and she is holding on and the women on the train are trying to help but they are pulling her this way and that way and her feet are dragging and she cannot hear what they are telling her to do because they are all talking at once and some of them are screaming, so she just lets go with a gasp and the last thing she sees is her jewellery kit, all split open, sending her tools and her tiny bright beads of jade and agate and amber tumbling into the air like clouds of holi powder, blessing her as she is dragged down.

Ladli walks to work now, even in the winter. She tells her husband that she prefers walking to catching the train to work, which is what everyone else in her neighbourhood does. At first he thought her preference was foolish and teased her for it, but now he leaves her be.

Even though Ladli has been told the trains are safer here in England than those back home, she does not trust them still. She does not trust the automatic doors and the passengers who do not meet her eye and the way everyone packs in together tightly and she is scared of the speed at which the train passes by and flaps her coat and steals her breath, so close that if she were to reach out her hand she might touch a grimy carriage in its flight.

So Ladli walks an hour each way every day instead, to the big department store in the centre of town where she spends her days with a thread laced between her teeth, leaning over women with flawless foreheads who think nothing of paying expensive sums of money every fortnight to have their already thin eyebrows arched this way and that. It is not a bad job. It is better than her first job, where she cleaned rich Indian businessmen's houses for pittance while their wives watched on, big carpeted houses with gold mirrors hanging on the walls and bathrooms attached to every bedroom. The wives gave her crumpled £5 notes, just a few, for all her hours of work and it crushed her inside.

It was a job that made her feel first ashamed and then later made her cry. Her family was not rich but even so she would never have had to do this for a living in India, she said to her husband in between wiping the tears staining her face.

Sometimes, teenage girls come to Ladli in the department store on Saturday mornings in pairs, texting and talking to each other about boys. Although Ladli does not understand everything they are saying, they talk so quickly and her English is still slow and unsteady, she understands their youth and recognises their vanity. The girls breeze in and out in tight tops and fitted jeans and headphones dangling from their phones like leashes and Ladli envies them their small priorities, their wilful ignorance of a world that is far, far bigger than them, a world where in an instant everything can come crashing down and change.

After the accident, a photograph of Suki was hung on the wall of Ladli's childhood home, draped with garlands of white and red flowers as if she were finally a bride. But the photograph did not bring Ladli comfort. At night, Ladli could not sleep in the room she had once shared with her sister all her life.

She listened for Suki, for her shuffling under her sheets and the murmurs in her sleep and the steady rise and fall of her breath, but there was silence instead. Ladli stared at Suki's cold mattress which no one had yet thought to remove, and she stared at it for hours until her eyes turned too dry to keep open any more.

During these endless nights that seemed to last forever, she wondered what would have happened had she not been there that day, on the back of Sunil's bike. She wondered what would have happened if Suki had not stopped for those few, precious seconds, stunned and confused to see Ladli behind her with her hair loose and her arms wrapped around the waist of a boy. She wonders whether, if she had not been there, Suki might not have had to run so fast, so carelessly, for the train after all.

Ladli carried all these thoughts inside her, piling up like heavy bricks, one on top of the other. It was these thoughts that made her refuse to see Sunil, telling him not to phone her any more. It was these thoughts that made Ladli throw away her make-up and her magazines and all of her other frivolous things that Suki complained about for so long, saying they cluttered their shared room, keeping only the bracelets that Suki had made.

It was these thoughts, too, that made Ladli agree, when her father came to her one night with a plan for her to marry soon and move away to a country she had seen only in films, where she might find work and make money to send home and help them, but also, he said, help herself. In the absence of a son, it was Suki who contributed an income for the family.

Now that Suki was gone, it was Ladli's turn and he pleaded with her. She was his only hope; his job at the jewellers was uncertain now that Suki was no longer there and his debts were growing deeper every day with interest he could not afford. He had already found a man in England to be her groom; her husband would help her find work.

It was because of all of these thoughts, building up like bricks, that Ladli said yes, accepting of her fate and the responsibility that she had to assume. Her parents cried as the date of her departure came closer, saying they had lost not one daughter but two, but it was agreed that it was for the best, that this way Ladli could help them with their financial mess.

It has been eight years since Ladli left India and nine years since Suki died, leaving semi-precious beads sprinkled all over the dirty train tracks.

It was not easy for Ladli at first, adjusting to a husband she did not really know and a language she did not completely comprehend.

But with time, she found purpose and with purpose came a reason to stay. She sends money to her parents each month now, after she has shared a portion of her salary with her husband to help towards their household bills, and if there is anything left, she skims it aside to save for the baby she one day hopes to have.

She does not always tell her husband that she is sending her parents money, for he does not think it is still necessary. But Ladli feels like it is what Suki would do, so she continues.

Ladli, who once spent her days being idle, skipping college classes so she could spend time with Sunil, and ambitious only for a love marriage and an air-conditioned house, has worked almost every day since she arrived in the urban town on the outskirts of the big city where she now lives.

She has paid off most of her father's loans, sums of money he said he had borrowed from anonymous friends to settle the expense of organising Ladli's wedding and Suki's funeral, which she knows really are gambling debts, overloaded with interest which spiralled her father further and further into debt. There are other costs Ladli contributes towards too, like her mother's hospital bills or things that need fixing in their small house.

She is proud of what she has been able to provide. She gave her mother money to build a new kitchen, modern and clean and bright. 'You are like a son to me,' her mother told her, words justifying Ladli's existence so far away from home.

Ladli is not sure if her father has stopped gambling completely, even though he had promised her he would. She does not ask him directly. She would rather not know.

She talks to her parents often, over the Internet or on the phone and though she finds herself thinking of them and worries about their health, this distance is enough for her. When she thinks of her parents, she thinks of hardship and struggle and a grief which no one talks of and she feels pain all over again. This distance, she thinks, is enough.

She has visited her parents three times over these years. With each visit she has distanced herself further still, sometimes without even realising she is doing it.

It has surprised her, her feelings towards the place she was born. At first she missed her parents desperately but the last time she visited, she found herself longing to come back to the small terraced house she has made her home. She counts the days until she can return, crossing them out one by one in her head.

Now she makes excuses for delaying her visits, saying the airfare is too much, that it is more practical for her to stay and work and send them money than be there with them in person. But the truth is she does not like going back to India any more.

Her life in England may not be easy, but she prefers it to what she knew before. It is easier for her to stay here and carry on, busy with work and her husband, than to be back in her childhood home where the memory of Suki stands still, suspended in time.

On her walks to work, Ladli used to find herself thinking about how things might have been different if Suki had not slipped and fallen that day. She used to think about the big houses in the new compounds where Sunil said they might live, and she used to think of him when she first came to England. She used to find life unfair.

But it has been years since she has thought about these things now. She has come to understand that it is not worth wishing for fate to change once it has decided its course.

It has been years, too, since she last thought of Sunil. Ladli knows, with the sense that always follows an ill-fated, immature affair that they would have come to nothing. He was no great love. He was just a boy.

She knows her husband cares for her and though it has taken time for her to understand him and his ways, for his upbringing was so different to hers, she has grown to care for him too, and together they have worked honestly and hard to create a future together.

They may not have luxury or wealth like Ladli had always enviously dreamed of, but they get by and the only real debt to their name is a mortgage on their small home which is manageable between the two of them.

Ladli used to wish for money, lots of it, resenting those that had it and resenting her father too for not making more and for getting them into difficulty in the first place. But she knows now, from the debts she has spent several years paying off, how destructive it can be and how the promise of money lured her father to a dark place from which he will never entirely be free.

So she is careful with her own money now, placing cash in envelopes hidden in the house, labelled carefully the way Suki used to do too. Still, sometimes as she is walking home, Ladli stops at the small newsagent for snacks and while she is there, about to pay, she secretly asks for a scratch card or two.

She prays for a quick win that never comes, and then she curses herself for it, vowing never to do it again as she throws it away.

8

Crushed

A mole that looks like a dark chocolate drop rests slightly above Miss Lewis's clavicle. It looks like a careless smudge of cocoa, escaped unseen from a mixing bowl, transferred accidentally by a hand tucking a stray strand of hair behind an ear. It looks as if Miss Lewis might have spent the morning baking brownies or some other such sweet things, instead of teaching French in a classroom on an autumn day.

She is not sure why but the tiny mole is all Keerat can think about, even though she is trying hard to concentrate in the classroom. The mole, the way it dances around every time Miss Lewis moves, keeps distracting her from past participles and formulations of the conditional tense.

She can hear Miss Lewis rehearsing and repeating verbs in the background. 'I would like,' she says, first in English, then in French. 'He, she, it would like. We would like.'

Keerat blinks her eyes for a little longer than necessary to try and focus on the class again. But the bell has rung and Keerat realises that she has spent the whole lesson in a daze.

'J'aimerais vous souhaiter une bonne fin de semaine,' Miss Lewis says to everyone, bringing her class to an end. 'Have a good weekend.'

'Thanks Miss Lewis,' says Keerat, as she passes by the front desk. 'Merci, Mademoiselle Lewis.'

Miss Lewis smiles at Keerat, as she packs up her notes. Miss Lewis does not look old enough to be a teacher. She looks like she might simply be someone's older sister, visiting from university, just passing through to pick a younger sibling up at the end of the day.

She is pretty and fresh faced; her skin is healthy in the way of someone who voluntarily opts to spend time outdoors. Miss Lewis looks like a version of the actress who plays the girl-next-door character on the serious American teen drama Keerat has been watching on satellite television, the girl the two male characters think is just a friend before realising, only too late, that she is the one they have each been in love with all along.

Sometimes, Miss Lewis twists her hazelnut-coloured hair into a loose knot with a band she keeps around her wrist. Often, she pops the band out of her hair with her fingers when she is seated behind her desk while trying to explain something complex about irregular verbs, looping it absent-mindedly around her thumb. When she sits at her desk marking homework or tests, her feet casually slip out of the back of her flat shoes as if she is at the beach, or barefoot in the garden. There are times Miss Lewis looks confused at the questions in the French grammar textbook, like she is not the teacher at all but a student herself again.

These gestures reinforce Miss Lewis's youth, her lack of expertise at finding herself in a classroom, but they are endearing to her students, who think she is the most wonderful teacher they have had during their school years.

It is not surprising that since she is young and easy-going in class, Miss Lewis has become popular among the students. She talks to them not just about French grammar but about movies, music, make-up. Once, one of the girls asks her if she has a boyfriend. She blushes and says no. 'There was someone. But we're not together any more.'

Keerat thinks Miss Lewis's ex-boyfriend must have been a fool to have left her. 'What an idiot,' she says later, while discussing Miss Lewis with her best friend Emily. They both agree Miss Lewis is the nicest teacher they have ever had.

It is late spring. The trees that line the curve of the cul-de-sac where Keerat lives are pink with blossom leaves, heartshaped like blotted lipstick kisses on crumpled tissue paper.

Sunlight falls into Keerat's bedroom in warm patches, dappling the wall and the carpet upon which she sits cross-legged. Emily sits opposite her, their revision notes spread out in front of them even though it is a Saturday.

The exam season is approaching. Keerat and Emily have been revising together over weekends and school holidays for months, making identical colour-coded record cards as memory prompts.

Emily and Keerat have been best friends for five years, ever since they started secondary school. Emily was the first person Keerat spoke to on their first day of school, where they were seated in alphabetical order by surname. Emily James, Keerat Jatt. They spent the first day side by side in every class, and have been more or less inseparable ever since.

Keerat's parents have certain rules. School work always comes first. Keerat is not allowed to go to sleepovers or school parties, but they make allowances for Emily. They like Emily. She is a good influence.

Emily is studious, like Keerat, and her parents have holidayed in India and say Sat Sri Akaal whenever they come to pick Emily up. Emily is not into things like flirting or boys. So Keerat is allowed to sleep over at Emily's house and Emily is equally always welcomed at Keerat's house.

Today, they are revising French. There is a test next week, a practice paper ahead of their final exam, and it matters to Keerat that she does well.

This is not unusual. It has always mattered to Keerat that she does well at school. Unlike her cousins, who are more interested in football than studying, she does not find it difficult to motivate herself for school.

Her father, the owner of a wholesale food factory, is always telling her to work hard. 'It is okay to be the owner of a factory,' he often says, while driving her to school. 'But not to work in one.'

She listens carefully to her parents when they say things like this. She thinks the world of them. She does not begrudge them any of their rules, because she agrees with the things that they say, about education being important, about how it is imperative that she should go to university and study for a degree.

There are only a few years left, and she will finally be there. University is her ultimate aim and because of this quiet, determined ambition, she has always taken great care preparing for exams and tests, even practice ones like the French one they have next week.

Keerat and Emily have been revising all morning. They have been memorising set phrases to scatter in the short essay they will be required to write, testing each other on vocabulary, writing out flowery, cleverly constructed sentences practising the use of the pluperfect tense.

But Emily is beginning to get impatient. She is picking at the nail polish on her toes while Keerat chants five different ways to introduce a sentence expressing an opinion in formal French.

Emily sighs and stretches back, her arms over her head. 'Don't you think we've done enough for today? I feel like my head is going to explode.'

Keerat frowns, her head bowed over the cards in front of her. She is not sure they have covered everything. She points out there are still two more grammar exercises in the textbook at the end of the chapter they are currently working their way through.

'It's just a practice test,' Emily says. 'I'm sure we've done enough. Don't worry so much, you'll do fine. We both will.'

'I hope so,' Keerat says. She pulls her hair band out of her hair, stretches it across her fingers the way Miss Lewis does. 'I just really want to do well in this test.'

Emily laughs. She is still lying flat, her hands resting on her stomach now. 'You always do well, Keerat. Besides, it's French. Miss Lewis loves you, silly.'

'No, she doesn't,' Keerat shakes her head, bashfully. She doesn't tell Emily that it's precisely because it is French, because it is Miss Lewis's subject, that she wants to do extraordinarily well in this test.

She doesn't know why, particularly, but for some reason she feels she wants to make Miss Lewis proud. She doesn't say this out loud because she is aware that it sounds strange and slightly stupid. Keerat works hard to make her parents proud, and it is not as if Miss Lewis is remotely like them at all.

But Emily is on her feet now, fiddling with Keerat's stereo and turning the volume up on a pretty song with lyrics about stars and lovers in the summertime. Emily pulls Keerat up from the carpet and they dance, ridiculously, in her room.

Later, before Emily has to go home, the girls eat sandwiches in front of the television in the conservatory. Keerat has been taping the American drama that everyone at school talks about, and there is an episode they have not yet seen ready to be watched, which she has saved as a treat for finishing French revision. 'There she is,' says Emily with her mouth full. 'The Miss Lewis lookalike.'

The actress that looks like Miss Lewis is about to be kissed. It is meant to be her first kiss with the boy she has secretly been in love with. Keerat and Emily watch intently, concentrating.

When the episode has finished and Emily has gone home, Keerat packs up her notes. She forgets for a while about the French test and about doing well for Miss Lewis's sake, pushing it to the back of her mind.

She spends the evening with her family. Her uncle and her aunt come over for dinner with her cousins, as they always do on weekends. She plays computer games with her cousins, Nav and Haroop, who are like brothers to her in the absence of any other siblings. They tease her, calling her square for spending her entire Saturday studying.

After dinner, they are about to put on an Indian action film that Haroop brought with him but Nav presses play on the video recorder before realising that there is still a tape inside. Keerat's drama comes up on the television screen. He laughs some more. 'Can't believe you watch this girly rubbish! Oh, kiss me, kiss me!' he pretends to swoon.

Keerat swats him around the head and quickly ejects the tape. 'I am a girl, idiot,' she reminds him. 'So I can watch this girly rubbish.' Haroop tells them both to be quiet and then eventually they settle down.

The action film they watch is typically Indian, with over-exaggerated villains and impossibly glamorous girls who need saving. 'Oi oi,' says Nav, whenever one of the actresses appears on screen, making some sort of comment about how attractive they are. Keerat rolls her eyes at him, but she too has to admit that some of these Indian actresses are the most beautiful women she has ever seen.

After they have left and her parents have gone to bed, Keerat pushes the tape with her American drama on it back into the machine. She lowers the sound, and then rewinds to the scene of the first kiss, to the moment where the girl who looks like Miss Lewis shuts her eyes and sways closer to the boy who settles his hands upon her shoulders.

Keerat is not sure why she is watching this again, but she pauses the kiss and presses the slow motion button on the remote. She is mesmerised.

Keerat has never been kissed. She has never been alone with a boy, other than her cousins. Keerat isn't that bothered about not having or having a boyfriend. Some of the other girls at school are always trying to impress boys by wearing short skirts and make-up, but Keerat and Emily have both agreed that that isn't the way they would like to be.

Keerat knows that one day, after she has completed her degree, she will get married. Her parents will start looking for a match for her, just like her uncle and aunt are looking for Haroop right now. She quite likes the idea of leaving it to her parents to decide. She thinks it will make things easier for her rather than trying to find someone on her own. It is no big deal to Keerat. It is the way things are done.

But, still, she would like to know what it might feel like to be kissed. She is not sure if she could wait until she is married to find that out.

Keerat is glued to the screen. She watches the girl who looks like Miss Lewis being kissed. She watches the girl and the way that she moves and the shadows that fall on her face as the boy standing opposite her leans in, and she does not know why, but she cannot take her eyes away.

On the day of the French test, when Keerat hands her paper in to Miss Lewis, which she ends up doing exceptionally well in, she ends up thinking of the kissing scene from the drama for a fraction of a second once again.

She does not know why or how the image of the actress who looks like Miss Lewis has come back into her head seemingly out of nowhere for just a few fragile seconds, and she blushes, blinking her eyes for longer than necessary to fade the image away. She tries not to think about it again.

Keerat picks up a brush and runs it through her hair. She notices her hands are trembling. She feels frenetic. She is not scared, exactly, but she is excited and nervous all at once. She feels like she wants to do something boundless only she doesn't know what, like laughing out loud or running as fast as she can, or doing star jumps on the spot, only she also knows that would be strange, so she doesn't do any of these things at all. Instead, she takes a deep breath and opens the door to her room and waits.

Haroop told her to do this before he left. He said it was the way he made friends at university on his first day. So Keerat is doing the same and she leaves the door open while she starts to unpack.

Her mother wanted to unpack for her, but Haroop and Nav convinced her it was best to let Keerat do it herself. Her mother cried when she left Keerat in her small, rectangular university bedroom, and her father looked mournful. Keerat too had tears in her eyes, but she had made Nav promise not to let her cry.

Only Haroop and Nav seemed happy, giving her big bear hugs before they left and whispering in her ear to go out, have a drink and let her hair down. 'Live a little,' Nav said, winking. She shoved him away, pretending like he was being stupid but secretly heeding his advice. She planned to at least try.

Keerat opens one of her boxes, packed with photos and books and CDs. There are some things she has planned to stick up on the wall. A photograph of her and Emily, a card wishing her all the best from Miss Lewis.

Keerat is studying for a degree in business studies with French and before she left school, she told Miss Lewis she would never have chosen French if it hadn't been for her. Keerat said she couldn't thank her enough and Miss Lewis hugged her, told her that was why she had become a teacher in the first place. Keerat remembers this as she tacks Miss Lewis's card to the pinboard fixed above the desk.

'Hi. Do you have plans for tonight? Want to come out with a bunch of us?' Keerat turns around. An Indian girl with shiny black hair and red lipstick is standing in the doorway. She smiles.

'I'm Anita,' she says. 'I'm in the room next door.' Anita looks behind her into the hallway and then squeals. 'I'm so glad there's another desi girl in this corridor! We're going to have a lot of fun,' she says knowingly.

It does not take long for Keerat to realise that Anita is everything she is not. Anita is flirtatious, a party-lover. Anita loves to dance, hates to study. She wakes up early before lectures, not to read through notes or prepare the way Keerat does, but to blow dry her hair and paint her nails.

She is the sort of girl Keerat has seen in the Asian parts of her hometown. The sort of girl her mother warns her about. Anita is loud, flamboyant, attention-seeking and dresses in clothes that are expensive but make her look ever so slightly cheap. She wears far too much perfume and is always in high heels. She hugs everyone. She is fun. She is so different from Emily, from anyone that Keerat has known before. Quickly, Keerat realises she loves being Anita's friend.

Since their rooms are right next to each other, it is inevitable that Anita quickly takes Keerat under her wing. Anita takes one look at the student societies Keerat has signed up for, debating and future entrepreneurs, and automatically signs her up to Asian social groups without even asking.

A few days after they have moved in, Anita is lying on Keerat's bed and points up at the photograph of her and Emily. 'Who's the gori?' she asks. Anita finds it hilarious when Keerat says it is Emily, her best friend. 'Okay,' she says. 'We seriously need to get the coconut out of you.'

Keerat is bemused. She has never thought of herself as anything but Indian. But Anita teases her and sees her as posh, as wanting to be white. She can't believe that Keerat doesn't have Indian friends, that there weren't that many Indian girls at her school. Anita promises to take her out. 'I'll show you your roots,' she laughs.

Anita is the kind of friend Keerat has never had before. She is nothing like Emily. She knocks on Keerat's door then enters without waiting.

She drags Keerat out to student clubs even when Keerat resists and says she needs to work. She lends Keerat clothes, the kind of clothes Keerat would never normally wear, and does her make-up for her. She compliments Keerat, forever telling her she looks cute.

In their first week, she buys Keerat her very first drink, then promises to get her drunk. She takes control of Keerat's social life, buying tickets for Indian dance nights where she introduces Keerat to boys who don't hesitate in placing a hand on her thigh.

Anita teases Keerat about one of these boys, a thin boy called Ravi who studies computer science. She keeps telling her Ravi likes her and Keerat thinks she might like him too.

Ravi always pays Keerat special attention, complimenting her eyes and her hair, and she likes it, loves it really, but she has wished for a long time that he would just hurry up and kiss her. They are never alone, though, because Anita is always there.

Anita doesn't attend all of her lectures. She points out she doesn't have to, because it is not as if their attendance is marked. So she convinces Keerat to skip some too, and they end up spending mornings in the student café, not doing very much at all.

When Keerat's parents phone on her new mobile phone, Anita presses the disconnect button and finds it funny. Anita is what Keerat's parents would call a bad influence, but Keerat doesn't mind. Keerat is in awe of Anita. She thinks she is resplendent.

Keerat's parents miss their daughter terribly. But they are patient. They understand when term-time progresses and Keerat says she can't come home on the weekends because she has to work. They miss her, but they are proud of their only daughter, working so hard.

In the beginning, Keerat feels bad about lying to them but it soon becomes easy for her to invent excuses and find reasons to stay at university on weekends so that she can go out. Anita finds it hilarious that Keerat is supposed to speak to her parents every day. Keerat is surprised that Anita's parents aren't strict. She thought every Indian family was.

Anita says her parents don't care. 'My parents have low expectations of me,' she laughs. Anita doesn't talk much about her family.

In the second term, Emily comes to visit. When Emily arrives at the train station, Keerat is pleased to see her after so long and tells her she has plans to take her out and show her Saturday night.

Emily is surprised. She has never heard Keerat talk like this. She had hoped to catch up, a quiet night talking over takeaway and maybe a film once they had finished sharing each other's news. But when they get back to halls, Anita is waiting and she is telling Keerat and Emily to hurry up.

Later, as they sit uncomfortably in a bar on stools that are damp from spilled drinks, packed awkwardly around a table that is too small, Emily is horrified when she sees Anita hand Keerat a drink. She stares at Keerat when Ravi comes up behind her to greet her by placing his hands around her waist and nuzzling her neck.

Emily takes Keerat aside. 'What's got into you?' she asks. Keerat steps back and asks Emily what she means.

'This,' Emily gestures all around her. 'This isn't you at all. Who was that boy?'

Keerat bats the question away, says Ravi is just a friend.

But Emily is furious. 'What would your parents say?'

Keerat throws her head back. Suddenly, she is annoyed at Emily and her righteousness. 'Fuck. My. Parents.'

Emily takes an early train back, leaving a note under Keerat's door. It says, 'You've changed. I don't think I like who you've become.'

Keerat crumples the note when she sees it in the early hours. She thinks what will be will be. Anita says that all the time. Jo hona hai, woh hona hai.

Despite Ravi's tactile affection, Keerat has still never been kissed. One night, she tells Anita. Anita laughs and says she cannot believe it.

She says she thinks it is sweet that Keerat is so innocent. She says she will tell Ravi to hurry up and the thought of finally being kissed makes Keerat feel dizzy, little bubbles rising up inside her one by one.

Keerat is lying slumped at the edge of Anita's bed. She looks up. 'So, what's it like,' she asks quietly, 'to be kissed?'

Anita kneels in front of her and places her hands gently on the sides of Keerat's face.

'This,' she says.

It happens so quickly that Keerat is too surprised to register how it feels. Afterwards, Anita stands up and acts as if it was nothing, as if kissing her was as normal as lending Keerat some of her clothes. Keerat doesn't know what to do, but she doesn't want to seem embarrassed if Anita is not, so she pretends like it was normal too.

Later that week, Keerat and Anita are in the bar. 'Do you know,' Anita says to some of the Indian boys who meet them for weekly drinks. 'I was Keerat's first kiss. I've taught her well.'

The boys jeer, asking Anita if Keerat was any good, offering to teach Keerat some more, then nudging Ravi sharply in his side. Ravi doesn't laugh like the others do. Instead he looks at Keerat with dismay and moves further away. Keerat is horrified. She is burning up inside.

She takes Anita aside and asks her to stop, but Anita doesn't care. 'Oh come on,' says Anita. 'It's just a bit of fun. It's not as if it actually meant anything.'

Keerat feels a stab of hurt and turns away. Anita shouts at her, incredulous. 'Don't tell me you actually thought it meant something!'

Tears roll down Keerat's face and they sting through her skin as she walks away. When she reaches her room, she locks her door so that Anita can't walk in unannounced. She keeps it locked whenever she is in for weeks.

At first, Anita thumps on the wall dividing their room, plays music deliberately loud to try and get Keerat to come out. She leaves notes under Keerat's door saying it was all just a joke, sends her messages on her phone, promising to sort things out between her and Ravi.

But Keerat does not understand any of it. She does not understand why Anita even kissed her at all. The longer Keerat avoids Anita, the more Anita stops trying to make things right until eventually, she stops trying at all.

Keerat starts to go home to her parents on weekends instead of staying at university and going out. But she is changed. They notice she is quieter all the time, as if she is lost in her own private world.

Nav is concerned and asks her if everything is okay. He asks her if someone has hurt her, if it is something to do with a boy, telling her she can talk to him. Keerat touches his arm lightly and shakes her head.

'No. No, it's nothing to do with a boy,' she says.

It is the final term of her first year. Keerat has not been able to avoid Anita completely. It is impossible, living in rooms right next door. Once, when Anita happened to be coming out of her room when Keerat was going in to hers, Anita looked at her with an expression of disgust, muttering 'dyke' below her breath.

The word pierced Keerat, stung her like a blistering antiseptic burning her skin. Keerat is sure she can't be what Anita says she is, but then there are days she doesn't know anything any more.

Mostly, though, whenever Keerat happens to be in the hallway or the communal kitchen at the same time as her, Anita looks right through her as if she is not even there. It makes Keerat feel sick. She stays in her room whenever she can and stares at herself in the mirror, wondering what is wrong with her.

Keerat had spent all of her time with Anita, and the few friends she made were all Anita's friends too. She never sees Ravi any more. Now that she is no longer friends with Anita, she is alone all the time.

Keerat has overheard Anita making plans to move into a student house with some other Indian girls. Keerat has no one to move in with, so she is reapplying to live in halls even though she does not want to and just wants to stay at home. She wants to drop out of her course, take a year off, start again. But she knows she can't let her parents down like that.

Sometimes, Keerat's heart races at night and it is all she can do to breathe. At times likes these, she places her palm on the wall that divides her room from Anita's and it is the only way she can calm down.

Keerat is not surprised when she learns she has failed her exams. But it is a shock to her parents. They are devastated and they look at Keerat, perplexed, when they open the letter from the university explaining the process for resits.

But Keerat does not talk about it. In fact, she has mostly stopped talking to them at all. She hardly eats her food, and her face is blank these days as if her spirit has left her.

Her parents try to reassure her and tell her it will be all right, if she sits her exams again. 'Beti, what went wrong? You always seemed to be working so hard,' her parents say. 'Has it been too difficult for you? What can we do to help?'

Keerat thinks her parents are too kind to her. She cannot take their concern. Whenever they try to talk to her, whenever her mother places a hand softly on her shoulder or her father smiles at her or brings her chocolates to cheer her up, she turns away or drifts like a ghost out of the room.

She thinks she would prefer it if her parents would shout at her or slam doors, tell her that she was a let down or a failure. She thinks to herself, dryly, that is what Asian parents are supposed to do. But they are too kind to her. And it is too much for Keerat to take. They do not insist on her taking her resits.

Keerat spends most of the summer holidays alone in her room. Sometimes she tries to make sense of it all and thinks about Anita and Emily and Ravi and even Miss Lewis until she can't think any more and somehow falls asleep.

Her parents phone Emily, thinking it would do Keerat good to see her best friend, but Emily does not answer the phone. They talk to her uncle and aunt and to Haroop and Nav, and each of them agree to take it in turns to help.

But when they knock on Keerat's door to see if there is anything they can do, she ignores them all. Once her cousins come in without asking.

They lean against the wall while Keerat is in bed. Haroop is engaged now and he is busy, talking about the wedding. Nav stretches out a hand to touch Keerat's hair, a display of affection he has never showed before, but she quickly moves away. She turns away to face the wall and curls up on her side, slipping her headphones on instead.

Her mother starts praying for her at the gurdwara and at home. She is terrified and does not know what has happened to her only child. She asks Nav, quietly, if it is something to do with a boy. He says he does not know. One day, she returns from the temple with the priest and Keerat lies still as he chants prayers over her body. She can hear her mother crying as she watches.

But the prayers do not make Keerat's pain go away, or fill the emptiness she feels. Her father calls a family friend, a doctor, who asks if he can speak to Keerat alone. He gently closes the bedroom door and asks her if she can hear him. He tells her that he is talking to her as a doctor and that everything is confidential between them.

Keerat can hear the doctor and as he says the words 'breakdown' and 'psychiatrist', tears form in her still, unblinking eyes. He stands up to leave and she suddenly grips his hand.

'Please,' she whispers. 'Help me.'

Keerat didn't go back to university that year. Her parents kept her at home to heal. There have been some difficult times, moments that were violent and hard to bear, when Keerat began to throw things and break things and hit people to let out a hidden rage. But Keerat sees a psychiatrist now. She has spent time in hospital and she is starting, slowly, to improve.

Her parents never ask her what she talks to the psychiatrist about. Though it hurts them that she cannot tell them, her own parents, how she feels, they can understand that speaking to a stranger is helpful for her.

The psychiatrist talks to Keerat about the feelings that crushed her and caused her to shut down. They talk about things like isolation and self-worth and, in one session, while Keerat is talking about Anita, the psychiatrist gently introduces the word sexuality.

'I don't know what you mean,' she says. Sexuality makes no sense to Keerat, she tells the psychiatrist. She has never had sex. She has only had one kiss.

But together, they begin to examine her past. She remembers Miss Lewis. She remembers watching films with Haroop and Nav and the beautiful girls on the screen. But she remembers too that she liked Ravi, and because Ravi is a boy she can't possibly be the things that Anita said she was, and at that point Keerat stops thinking at all, because she still does not know what any of it means.

Keerat has not seen Emily for over a year. She has thought, often, of writing a letter to her to explain that she has left university, that she has come home. But she is not ready to do so yet.

For now, she spends much of her time at home with her parents. She is better than she was and she is considering enrolling back into a business studies course, only this time one that is closer to home. She does not want to be far away.

Nav and Haroop often come over to keep her company. They are the only people of her age group that she sees. There are all sorts of things to plan for Haroop's wedding, and even Nav is being introduced to girls now too. One day, Nav is telling Keerat about the latest girl he has met, when he stops and looks at her sideways.

'Do you think you'll ever get married too? When you're feeling completely better?' he asks.

Keerat pops her band out of her hair and stretches it across her fingers. She shrugs her shoulders and shakes her head. She does not know if she will ever find someone who will accept the way she feels. Besides, there are days when she still does not even know what her feelings mean herself. It hurts her head to think about it too much, sometimes.

Her mother has on occasion mentioned the concept of inviting a few Indian families over to their house, families with eligible sons. But her father has held back and has said it is not the right time yet. At these times, Keerat stays quiet and does not say anything.

Keerat does not know if she will be happy with an Indian boy. She liked Ravi, but she remembers the way he looked at her in disgust when Anita talked about their kiss, and she is not sure if she will ever meet a boy, an Indian boy, who will accept her the way she is.

She cannot talk to her parents about any of this, because she feels like she still does not know who she is. Her psychiatrist has spoken to her about things like coming out, but even the words, coming out, do not make sense to her. Boys and girls, she likes them both. But how can she tell her parents, who are looking forward to one day finding her a husband, that? Sometimes she feels like there is no place for her.

This is what Keerat is thinking about, when Nav asks her if she thinks she will ever get married. And because she is so tired about thinking about it, all the time, alone in her head, she does not say anything to Nav. Instead, she starts to cry.

It is months before she can talk to Nav about the confusing, conflicting thoughts in her head. The psychiatrist has provided her with leaflets and booklets to read, and Keerat realises there are words and terms to describe how she feels, identities she can relate with.

One day, when Nav is talking to her about the girl he is seeing, Keerat interrupts, in a fumbling and quiet and not altogether clear way, and tells Nav she thinks she is perhaps both gay and straight. It is not a rehearsed speech, and years later she will not even remember the words she said, but at this moment, she manages to describe how she feels, the thoughts in her head, for the very first time.

Nav has never been so serious with Keerat before. He is quiet, but he does not shout at her and tell her it cannot be. He holds Keerat as she cries again.

He does not say anything. He does not judge. But he promises he will help her, when the time is right, to tell her parents. When she asks him if he thinks they will still love her, if they will still let her be a part of their life, he shakes her ever so gently with tears in his eyes. 'Of course they will,' he cries. 'Of course they will.'

A year later, Nav is getting married. Keerat is helping him plan for the wedding and so she is not surprised when Nav says he wants to show her photos of an Indian wedding he has seen. He clicks on his computer and shows Keerat the screen.

The bride is beautiful. Her hands are dark with burgundy henna and her sari is heavy with gold. She wears antique diamonds and ruby drops in her hair, around her neck, falling from her ears. She is breathtaking, Keerat thinks.

But then Nav clicks again, and shows her another bride, an American woman in a mountainous white dress. She too wears a ruby drop in her hair and inches of bangles around her wrists.

It takes Keerat a moment to realise that the brides are marrying each other. Then she sees family in the photos too, the Indian bride carried by her brothers who look like princes in embroidered shalwar kameez.

The photos make Keerat smile and then suddenly she feels overwhelmed. Tears form in her eyes, and though she cannot put words to it at that moment, later, when she looks at the photos again, she realises she feels sad because she is not sure she could ever imagine doing the same.

But Nav touches her hand. He tells her it is time to tell her parents. 'It won't be easy, Keerat. But it's not impossible,' he says and at this moment, Keerat finally feels understood.

9

At the opposite end

She is walking barefoot along the beach at Oyster Bay. Her flimsy sandals dangle from her little finger, the soles of her feet leaving vanishing imprints in dusty white sand.

She is arm-in-arm with her college girlfriends. They walk, looped together like bracelet links. They walk like this up and down the beach, up and down. They throw back their hair and they laugh. They are young and they are exuberant and they are beautiful.

It is the summer of 1964 and Tanzania is still newborn. The sunset is golden. There is hope, everywhere.

She notices him first. He is with a loud group of boys. They are lounging on white plastic chairs which they have set down in the sand to face the ocean, eating cones of groundnuts and sipping khungu juice from paper cups.

He is wearing a white shirt and brown trousers. His sleeves are rolled up, his collar unbuttoned. He leans back in his chair and unlike the other boys who are laughing loudly and posing in order to command attention from the various groups of girls walking along the beach, he is simply sitting and looking out far away at the waves, lost in his thoughts.

She notices him not just because he is breathtakingly handsome, with film-star-thick hair, a noble profile and a scatter of stubble across his jaws, but because he does not behave like the other boys he is with. She notices him because he looks like he is dreaming, staring out at the ocean, and she is a dreamer too.

She watches him for a short while, considering the contours of his face. 'I know him,' one of her college girlfriends whispers in her ear. 'He is a friend of my brother's. He has come to my house. I can introduce you.'

The connection is an unremarkable coincidence as somehow all the Indian families seem to be connected in one way or the other in Dar es Salaam, but she believes it is fate, a higher force, that has brought them together.

They are introduced. 'Rochan, Shreeya. Shreeya, Rochan.' She steadies herself. 'Of course it's you,' she thinks. 'But of course.' In an instant, she feels like she knows him already.

This is how she falls in love, in a split second standing in front of the ocean and the sinking sun, barefoot in the sand, his name and hers forever repeating in her mind.

Ever since Patrick broke up with her, Reema has arrived at work early every day. It is a first for her; usually she is one of the last to arrive and only just makes it in time, as the daily shop floor and sales briefing is about to start.

But since Patrick broke up with her, she has been there an hour and a half before the store opens its doors. Other than Shreeya, the strange little old Indian lady who works on the same floor, she is almost the only sales assistant there so early. This break-up has done wonders for her work ethic, she thinks.

Reema hasn't been able to sleep for two months, since Patrick came round to her shared flat that night for dinner. She remembers most details about that night, only up until the point at which he pushed away her hands and said 'I don't want to do this any more.' After that everything else is a blur.

That day, she had gone down to the Foodhall in her lunch hour and bought a dinner-for-two meal deal, carefully selecting a main and two sides and a box containing two slices of New York cheesecake for dessert. Patrick did not often come to hers. Even though her flatmate Holly was hardly ever there, Patrick, who was past the stage of sharing a flat with others, preferred not to have anyone else around. Besides it was always easier, he said, for her to stay round his instead because most nights he had to work late. Since he came to hers so rarely, Reema felt it was special on the occasions he did.

She was changing out of her work clothes when he arrived, quietly letting himself in with the keys he hardly ever used. She was telling him something entirely mundane about the meal deal she had bought, her voice muffling in and out as she pulled her top over her head.

But he kept interrupting her, saying they needed to talk, and then by the time she'd sat down, he somehow managed to smash her heart in two as carelessly as if it were a dinner plate. She doesn't quite remember what happened next, but then soon he was gone.

The salmon en croûte she had so considerately selected turned black in the oven, and the garlic butter potatoes stayed in their flimsy plastic box for days until Reema realised they were about to reach their best-before date. Then, she took a fork, and pierced the film top with sharp short angry stabs, wiping her cheeks with the back of her hand with every set of holes she punched.

Now, Reema doesn't sleep. She lies there, thinking of nothing, waiting for an acceptable time to start her day which is usually just before six o'clock, in time for breakfast television to begin.

Then, she gets out of bed, showers and brushes her teeth. She dresses in something smart and shop-floor appropriate. A skirt, a fitted shirt, flat shoes that she can walk in.

It helps her, having a daily routine, so that she doesn't have to think. She convinces herself that she is fine, doing all right, but she misses Patrick and the hurt she feels is pounding in her stomach and in her head, permanent blows of emptiness that thrash inside her, wave after wave.

It is easy for Shreeya to fall in love with Rochan. She has finished her studies and her older brothers and sisters, all six of them, have already long left for jobs in England, one by one. Her mother died years ago, her father is busy with work in his contractor business.

So, because she is alone and free from her family, Shreeya can spend the summer freely falling in love with Rochan. They fall in love under the palm trees that line the beach up at Oyster Bay and then continue, further along the shore.

They meet first in the company of others, at picnics and birthday parties and then, more daringly, at hotel beach parties where Shreeya dances in daisy-print bell bottoms with all of her friends, drawing Rochan's attention with her hair and her eyes and her smile.

Then slowly and more daringly still, they begin to meet alone. Being mostly on her own at home, Shreeya is bold, leaving notes for her father saying she is spending the day with this girlfriend or that, when really she is with Rochan all the while.

She is expected to join her older siblings in England. Her brothers and sisters have written letters to her father saying it is time for them to leave Tanzania too. 'Who knows what will happen to us Indians now that Tanganyika and Zanzibar have become one. You should leave now,' they write in their aerograms.

Her father briefly suggested they move to India, the country of his birth, but none of his children agreed. They have never been there. 'We will be more at ease in England,' her older brothers say.

But although it has been planned out for her, Shreeya is not ready to leave yet. 'I will go when you go,' she tells Rochan.

Rochan is going to start his own business and when his plans are finalised, he will go to London first.

'You must come with me,' he tells Shreeya. 'I will talk to my parents. We will leave together, husband and wife.'

Shreeya does not want to go to England and work like some of the other Indian women who have left Tanzania do. She has told Rochan this already; that their fortune will have to be made by him. Besides, her brothers will never allow her to work in a bank or be a teacher, jobs other families consider suitable for a woman.

'The women in my family,' she tells Rochan, 'we have never worked like that.' But Rochan says that is fine. He has promised he will provide for her. He will give her everything she needs.

Shreeya puts her head on Rochan's shoulder and looks out at the ocean. Her heart surges and she has that feeling, like something is about to happen.

'You have got to get over him. You have got to snap out of this,' says Yasmeen. 'It's been, what, a month? A month and a half? And you're like, misery, everywhere.'

She gestures with her hands, palms open, scanning Reema up and down. 'Misery. Everywhere. Look, I know you liked him. But he really wasn't worth it. If he really loved you, he wouldn't have left you. And besides, would it really have gone anywhere? Really? It's time to move on.'

Reema sighs. This is exactly why she comes to work, every day, she thinks. So she can fold towels and her best friend can tell her everything she already knows but doesn't want to think about.

'Yasmeen, please,' she says quietly. 'It's been two months. And I'm trying, okay? I'm really trying.'

Yasmeen reaches out her hand across the soft duck-egg towels which they are folding together into neat, thick bundles.

'I know. Just, you know. Try harder.'

Yasmeen and Reema met two years ago, when Reema first started work on the Soft Furnishings and Decorative Accessories Floor on

Level Two. Yasmeen, who had been working at the store since she left college, took it upon herself to show Reema the ropes, raucously whispering something about 'brown girls sticking together in a white place like this'.

Though Yasmeen is brasher and bolder than Reema in the way that she dresses and the way that she speaks, and though Yasmeen calls Reema a snob and a coconut because she went to private school and grew up in Surrey not Southall like she did, Reema likes her, a lot.

Since all of Reema's university friends have gone on to proper jobs, careers with promotions and prospects, she has lost touch with them. When in the past they have met up for dinner at upmarket Italian chains, they order freely and even when the bill is split it is often more than Reema can afford. It is easier, less embarrassing, to simply not be there.

So she spends much of her free time with Yasmeen, taking their brief lunch breaks together while at work, and when they are not on weekend shifts, sometimes they spend that time together too.

Reema's sales assistant position was only supposed to be a summer job. She was sure her degree in art history would eventually lead to something else. She applied to a few selective jobs in museums and art galleries for positions that she didn't really know much about but sounded nice, like heritage assistant or visitor experience leader, but either she never heard back from them or they turned out to be looking for volunteers.

Sometimes she had heard positions were filled by the nieces and nephews of managers higher up or in other departments, and slowly, she stopped searching at all.

But she likes it in the department store. For one, she gets paid. And for another, she genuinely enjoys her job. She likes talking to customers, watching them carefully for clues about what they might buy.

She imagines what sort of lives they lead, picturing their homes filled with products she can't afford but knows every detail of, expensive sheets and designer lamp shades and impractical silk cushions, all beautiful things to make beautiful homes.

It is, she thinks, as good as working in a gallery or a museum. She is surrounded every day by beautiful things.

It was in the store that she met Patrick, seven months ago. He looked confused, picking up flat-packs of bedsheets, his hair ruffled and damp from the rain outside. Reema thought he looked cute. Breathtakingly so.

'May I help you?' she asked. He didn't know anything about thread counts, he explained. He had just moved into a new flat, he said, and he wanted expensive sheets. It was time he stopped living like a student, he laughed. And she laughed with him, and helped him, showing him expensive duvet sets made from 400 thread-count cotton that felt like silk or satin in soft shades of grey.

'I wouldn't normally say this,' he said at the till. 'But can I buy you a coffee to say thank you for helping me?'

Sometimes, when it is quiet in the Bed and Bath Linen corner of the Soft Furnishings floor and there are not many customers around, Reema allows herself to think about Patrick. She wonders what she did wrong, what pushed him away. She wonders why she keeps making mistakes and why every relationship she has had always ends with her being left behind, never the other way round.

She thinks something must be broken inside of her to make everything turn out this way and she shakes her head, softly.

Sometimes, she replays the day she met Patrick in her head, until Yasmeen loudly interrupts her thoughts.

'Reema! He's a prick. Honestly, what sort of man cares about thread counts? I just don't get what you're so hung up about. Besides, you know it was never going to go anywhere. His name is Patrick. Try explaining that one to your family, hey.'

Reema is frequently taken aback by how Yasmeen can tell what's in her head.

'How do you know?' she asks. 'How do you know I was thinking of him?'

'Because,' says Yasmeen. 'It is written all over your sad, sorry, pathetic face.'

Then she sticks her tongue out at Reema and winks, as if to say she is only joking, that she doesn't think Reema is sad or sorry-looking or pathetic at all even though Reema knows, and Patrick probably must have known, that really she is all of those things, sad and sorry and pathetic all rolled into one.

Shreeya holds the piece of paper that she has been waiting for in her hands, and turns it over and over again. It is Rochan's note, the one he promised he would drop in the letterbox for her in the morning when her father would be at work, and Shreeya is reading each line carefully.

'It is not the outcome either of us are hoping for,' he writes. 'They do not believe in our castes marrying. I am sorry. I cannot think of what else to say. But please, trust in me. Believe me, I will find a way. I will contact you when I know more and have planned what to do. Please do not worry. I will think of something.'

She sits cross-legged on her bed, her braid falling over her shoulder and her heart feels heavy with dread and despair. She has not known romantic love before, so she has not known the heartbreak or the tension that comes with it and the pain is more physical than she had ever thought. Her chest tightens, it is hard for her to breathe and there is a cutting pain digging into her stomach, through her left side.

'But we have it all planned out,' she thinks to herself. 'So how can they just take it away?'

She does not want to start hating the people she already considers to be her in-laws. But already, they are making things difficult for her, judging her before they have even met her purely on the status into which she was born. There is no one at home, the servants are out on errands, so she sits on her bed and she cries as loudly as she likes.

When she has run out of tears, and her eyes feel itchy and dry, Shreeya sits still on her bed and keeps turning over the piece of paper scribbled with Rochan's hurried, panicked few lines. She turns it over, again and again, and she marvels at how quickly things can change.

She feels powerless because her fate is not in her own hands and it is not even with the gods but it lies shapeless and flat in the possession of Rochan's parents whom she has not even met yet.

But, she remembers, Rochan has promised her the world. She is sure that he will find it for her. All she has to do is wait.

Reema likes being in the department store alone, early in the morning. It gives her time to not have to think about anything. She likes the quiet, before her colleagues arrive or the customers come in.

The lighting is always soft, always flattering, and there is a hush that falls over Soft Furnishings and Decorative Accessories as the cleaners, who have been there for hours, finish polishing the floors. Reema thinks all the preparation makes the store feel like it is getting ready for a party or a wedding every day.

This morning, Reema is tidying up one of the beds on display, smoothing out and tucking in an Egyptian cotton and sateen set of sheets. She refolds layers of fine cashmere throws, draping then across the bed casually. She chooses three velvet cushions of different sizes and colours, strategically placing them in front of each other, the biggest at the back and the smallest at the front, like siblings lined up for a family photo. She glides her hand across the sheets one more time, checks the price tags and wonders what it would feel like to sleep so effortlessly in a bed so expensive, when Shreeya, the little old Indian lady that works on the same floor, approaches.

'You have done a good job,' she says slowly. 'You have an eye for the colours, perhaps you should ask to have a go at more styling.' Reema smiles sarcastically, thinking 'Yeah, right' in her head.

Most people, her brothers and her parents mainly, assume there is no skill involved in her job at all. In the beginning, they were quick to take advantage of her store discount, but then they started to tell her she was wasting time, looking at her with pity as if she had thrown all her choices away by choosing to work in a shop, as if they thought she had hundreds of choices to begin with.

When she still lived at home, before she had moved out in anger, she had seen her parents and her brothers exchange glances as if to say, 'But what else could she expect to do with an art history degree?'

She had seen her father look at her, calculating all the money he could have saved on her private school education if he had not sent her there in the first place. He wouldn't have, if only he had known that at the end of it all, this is what she would become. She had seen her mother look at her, utterly fed up, like she is not the daughter she had wanted her to be.

When she remembers these observations, she closes her eyes and counts to ten and reminds herself not to go there again. At those times, she tries to remember to breathe, just breathe, and she tries to remind herself that no matter how much of a failure her family have made her feel, she earns her own money and manages, however tightly, to pay her own rent and that is her own, small victory.

Anyway, it doesn't even matter, Reema thinks. They hardly see her now, because the disappointment she has become is too much for them to bear. Since the space between them is now so vast, Reema doesn't bother any more to follow their rules of no drinking and no drugs and no sex before marriage.

'What about loving your children unconditionally?' she thinks bitterly sometimes. 'What's your cultural stance on that?'

Shreeya is still talking to her, in her slow, rolling voice with pauses longer than necessary between her words. 'Are you okay, dear? I have seen you come in early every day lately,' she says.

Reema smiles again. Shreeya makes her feel nervous, mostly because Reema is never quite sure what to call her. For all her disassociation with the Indian rules and regulations her parents brought her up in, Reema can't quite let go of some of the small things, like taking off her shoes when she steps on the carpet or not leaving books on the floor.

Ordinarily, she would call an Asian woman of Shreeya's age Aunty, but she can't bring herself to do that in the department store in front of her colleagues and customers who might overhear. They wouldn't understand that Shreeya isn't really her Aunty at all and then they wouldn't understand why she calls someone she doesn't even know by a familial term in the first place. And so she avoids calling her by her name at all. On the rare occasions when she has required Shreeya's attention, she has stood awkwardly, waiting patiently for her to turn around, or loudly saying 'Um. Excuse me?' and then feeling quite stupid about it all.

Reema does not know much about Shreeya, other than she has worked at the store for longer than anyone else and should have retired years ago. Yasmeen calls Shreeya The GrandDaadi behind her back.

'I bet all the others think she's my granny just because she's brown,' she snorts. 'They probably think you're my cousin too.'

Now whenever Reema sees Shreeya, she pictures her dead grandmother in front of her and feels terribly ashamed.

Reema feels obliged to say hello because Shreeya is Indian and old and for some reason this makes her feel guilty. But she doesn't know what else to say. She doesn't want Shreeya to overhear the crass things Yasmeen says, or to know that they have both on occasion dated customers who have come into the store.

Shreeya is old and traditional and doesn't pronounce her vowels when she speaks. She is perhaps a little strange, or at least that is how she appears in the long kurtas and baggy trousers and cardigans she insists on wearing to work, and Reema feels sorry for her and her circumstances, of which she admittedly knows nothing, because she is an old lady who still has to commute every morning and work in this department store.

'I'm fine, yes,' replies Reema. 'I'm just trying to work harder, make a good impression I suppose.'

Shreeya nods and purses her lips by way of approval. 'Oh yes. We people, we work hard,' she says. 'It is a good quality we have.'

She is shaking as she positions the puloo of her sari on her shoulder. Rochan told her to meet him at the temple in the city, and although she has been preparing for this day for the last two weeks and, in some ways, ever since she first met him, Shreeya is not sure she is ready for it. She thought she was, all along, but now she does not know any more.

Rochan is certain the priest will marry them. 'He has given me his word,' he said. Priests did not care about caste, he said to Shreeya. 'They believe we are all equal, one and the same.'

But even then, as he told her of his plan, Shreeya trembled. She has packed a small bag to take with her, just as Rochan told her to. Once they are married they will travel to Moshi where Rochan's friend has booked them into a guesthouse with views of Kilimanjaro.

She is amazed by how calm Rochan appears; he is not concerned about his parents' reaction. 'Oh, they will calm down,' he says, when Shreeya asks him about them, as if his parents are just an afterthought. 'They just need time.'

But Shreeya is not so nonchalant. Something about what they are going to do, marrying in secret and running away, hoping that their families will eventually understand, does not feel right to her. Her instinct sits in the pit of her stomach like a puddle of oil, telling her she is making a terrible mistake.

Shreeya sits down, closes her eyes, counts to ten. 'Can I do this?' she asks herself. 'Can I leave my family in this way?' Her brothers and her sisters-in-law and her sisters are all waiting for her in London. She is supposed to be joining them within a month, her ticket is already booked. Her father will leave once the sale of his business is tied up and then he will shut up their house in Dar es Salaam for good. Their family will be together again.

But Rochan wants her to arrive in England with him as his bride. Friends of his have eloped before. 'It is not as difficult as you think,' he encourages her. He is carefree, devoid of responsibility to anyone but Shreeya and it scares her, how easily he thinks of running away.

And though it is romantic, and though it is in many ways everything Shreeya has always wanted, for she thinks she is a dreamer like Rochan too, it is also not the way she had expected it to be.

She glances at her watch. Rochan is waiting. She does not have long. She remembers to breathe, just breathe. She studies the photograph of her mother which she keeps on her dressing table and she closes her eyes once more, and counts to ten.

Then she unhooks her puloo, unwraps her sari and sits down, loosening her hair from her braid so that it tumbles around her shoulders in loose, weak waves.

Yasmeen flicks Reema's hair. 'Oi,' she says. 'I texted you last night. You didn't reply. So, how was your day off? Anything I should know?' she asks.

Reema looks up from the knitted gift blankets she is rolling up like chunky pastries and tying with ribbon.

'No,' she says, more sharply and curtly than she intended to. Yasmeen raises her eyebrows, noting the change in Reema's tone.

'Well, okay then,' she says, shrugging her shoulders as if to say that she was only trying to help, then backing away.

Reema feels momentarily bad for the way she just snapped at Yasmeen, but at the same time she doesn't really care. She has had enough of Yasmeen's constant attempts at tough love. She is bored of the same old routine, the one that insists her post-break-up blues have gone on too long, that she has to move on.

She wonders what Yasmeen would say, if she really told her how her day off had been. If she told her she didn't get changed out of her pyjamas all day because she didn't see the point, that she often feels like that most days. If she told her she turned off her phone and drew the curtains, then boiled an entire bag of pasta and ate the whole lot, all the while feeling ugly and fat.

She considers the look Yasmeen might have on her face, if she told her she logged into Patrick's email, because she knows his password and it hasn't occurred to him to change it yet. If she told her she saw messages from different girls who had contacted him through his apparently new online dating profile, calmly read and deleted them all before changing his password to lock him out of his own account.

She wonders what Yasmeen might think of her, if she told her that it wasn't the first time she'd done something like this, that it is far easier to do than it sounds.

She wonders whether Yasmeen would be able to think of anything at all appropriate to say, if she told her she kept hearing her family shouting at her in her head, telling her she is wasting her time and wasting her life in a dead-end job that is going nowhere. If she told her she considered picking up the phone and asking her mum to help her, please God help her, but thought her mum would never come.

She wonders whether Yasmeen would understand, if she told her she took painkillers for her head to make the voices go away and then ever so casually wondered what would happen if she took more. If she told her she had inhaled only the stale dry air of her flat. If she told her that when she finally fell asleep, she did so hating herself, again.

Rochan keeps calling Shreeya. It was easy to find out where she lived; he only had to ask any one of the Indian families recently arrived in London from Tanzania in order to track her family down.

He tells her repeatedly that he has forgiven her for not turning up at the temple. He says he understands her hesitations but that she needs to follow her heart and take risks. He says a life without risks is a life in monochrome.

Shreeya hears the hidden insult, that he thinks she is turning boring and dull, but it amazes and angers her in equal measures at how lightly he takes it all. How he considers this all to be a game, when every choice she makes could determine the entire path of her fate.

She cannot simply leave her family because the prospect of it is too huge, too much for her to do, and this is what she tells him constantly down the telephone.

Anyhow, her family knows about the planned elopement and they are not pleased. It did not take long for the news to leak out and then to spread. It almost does not matter that Shreeya did not go, that Shreeya did not marry Rochan in secret after all, because her family treats her as if she did. They are cold. Mostly, they are disappointed and it is the disappointment that makes Shreeya resolved to make them proud of her once more.

But Rochan sneers when she tells him this. He tells her she is a coward, a sheep. That she is not the dreamer, the free spirit, that he thought her to be.

'You are right,' she says. 'Perhaps I am not. Perhaps that is not me at all.'

She writes to Rochan, and tells him her instinct is telling her something is wrong, and that she has to trust herself more than she can trust him. She tells him to be free. Though she still loves him, she says goodbye.

Still, Shreeya cries herself to sleep every night for years. Sometimes, when her brothers seem angry with her for refusing the suitors they bring, she wonders whether she did the right thing. She hears, through their shared circle of friends, that he is engaged to be married now to a girl he met in India. It breaks her heart, millions of times.

On his wedding day, she sends him a telegram. 'I AM HAPPY FOR YOU,' it says.

The next morning while the cleaners are still polishing the floor, Shreeya appears at Bed and Bath Linen with a tray carrying two cups of tea and croissants in a paper bag from the canteen. 'Good morning *beti*,' she says.

Reema is surprised, smiling more than she needs, insisting on paying her back. It happens again the next day. And the next.

It is a strange morning ritual. They sip their tea mostly in silence. Occasionally Shreeya interrupts the hush of the store, passing an observation about new sheets or price changes. Reema can't think of anything to say at all. Then, when the others arrive in time for the morning briefings, Shreeya wanders off back to Rugs and Cushions.

Yasmeen laughs at Reema when she tells her. 'Probably wants to marry you off to her great grandson,' she says.

After four days of buying her tea, Reema pulls out her purse to pay Shreeya back.

'No, no,' says Shreeya, putting out a withered hand and pushing Reema's purse away. 'It is my treat. It is nice for me. But now, tell me why you are really here, so early in the morning every day looking like you are so sad and lonely. It is about a boy, isn't it? I can tell. I know that look. I have worn that look for a long time too. But when I am feeling down, I work as hard as I can. So I know you must be feeling down too. So, tell me.'

Reema pretends to laugh, as if there is nothing wrong. She mumbles excuses, saying 'No, no, it is nothing like that at all.'

But Shreeya will not let her go. 'No, beti. I can't watch you being sad. I know it is something to do with that boy who always came in here to talk with you. So you talk to me now. Tell me what's wrong.'

Reema gives up and looks down and quietly says she doesn't think Shreeya would understand.

'Try me,' Shreeya smiles mischievously. 'You might be surprised. I might be able to help after all.'

Life is not as lazy in London as it was in Dar es Salaam where they had servants to take care of everything. Shreeya had been warned about this.

She is expected to help her sister-in-law and her sisters in their neighbouring houses with their various chores. They moan all the time about how much there is to do. Shreeya wishes she could mute their voices, they turn her head numb. Everything feels listless.

'Why did we leave, then?' she thinks to herself. 'If all we are to do here is complain?'

She needs to get out of the house in East London. She needs to be able to breathe. At home, her brothers and her sisters pester her constantly about suitors, but she cannot think about any of that, not after Rochan.

Sometimes, she still aches for him. She thinks he may be the only man she could ever love. She tries not to think about his new wife, how his fingers might trail softly down her neck or trace her collarbone. She feels like she is living in a cage. Sometimes she is worried she might break, she might scream.

Shreeya desperately needs some relief. She is frustrated with spending all her time with her family so she phones around, hunting down old friends who had moved from Tanzania too. They start to meet regularly and it gives her something to look forward to.

One time, one of them casually mentions a department store she has shopped in. 'They want to make money out of Diwali. They want Indian girls in colourful saris to sell candles,' she says. 'Who wants to do it?'

It sounds absurd. Shreeya thinks it is the easiest job she has ever heard of. 'Me,' she says. 'I do.'

Shreeya has not worn a sari since the day she was supposed to get married. But it is fun, dressing up in the staff room of this glamorous store, with her friends. It feels like they are getting ready for a wedding, or a party, for each of the five days they are meant to be there.

Some of the other girls are shy when the customers approach, anxious of the questions they might be asked. But Shreeya feels like she hasn't felt this comfortable since she danced on the sand in front of the Bahari Beach Hotel back in those easy, lazy days in Dar es Salaam. It comes so easily to her, talking to rich English customers with money to spend on luxuries like expensive candles that smell of roses and herbs and have little to do, really, with Diwali at all.

On the last day of her brief employment, Shreeya is taken aside and led to the office of the manager. He welcomes her in, smiles at her and pours her a china cup of tea. His family owns the store, he says. He is always looking for talent.

'A sales position is an important role. You are very good at selling,' he says. 'You have a magnificent smile. Are you in need of a job, at all?'

Reema had never imagined telling anyone about the dark, frightful things that hide inside her. Some of it is to do with Patrick but not all of it and that is what scares her the most. That all the other feelings, the ones about her wasting her life away, might never go away.

Yasmeen tells her to pull it together and to move on, but it occurs to Reema now that no one has ever simply asked her what's wrong. And as Shreeya stands in front of her, offering her a way to unload in a way nobody has, it is hard for Reema not to crumple and not to cry and not to say, 'Aunty, I have made too many mistakes. I don't know what to do any more.'

But Reema looks at Shreeya's elderly face, crinkled and ruched like soft worn cotton washed hundreds of times, and she is sure that this little old Indian lady couldn't possibly understand.

How could she? She is in her seventies, from a different place and a different time. So Reema shakes her head and says, 'Nothing, nothing wrong at all.'

Shreeya has worked in the store for fifty years, and she can read people quickly, like thin, flick-through magazines. So she knows that Reema is lying. And she knows why. She knows Reema thinks Shreeya is just a little old Indian lady with no knowledge of the real world.

Shreeya smiles, bemused that these youngsters find people of her age so judgemental, when really they are the ones making all the assumptions first.

Reema has not thought to ask Shreeya about how she ended up here, in Rugs and Cushions. If she did, she would know that Shreeya has worked in every department and now, she has the pick of the store. She could have been a buyer and moved up the ranks, as the manager who first recruited her begged her to do every year until he died, but she refused. 'I like people. I like talking to them on the shop floor,' she said. 'I will stay right here.'

At first Shreeya's brothers were not impressed. No woman in their family had ever worked before. But her sisters were enchanted by the things she brought home from the store, reams of silk leftover from Haberdashery, large platters discarded from China & Glass because of tiny, invisible chips that no one could see. There were bonuses and commissions too, all because Shreeya knew how to sell fanciful rugs to royalty and skirts to actresses to wear to their premieres.

Quickly, it became a great thing, her job. It bought her a flat, and with it independence and the courage to live alone. Finally, her family understood that what they wanted for her, marriage and children, was not the life she chose and nor was it what she needed.

Now, she has nestled in Rugs and Cushions, where it is slightly quieter. She takes the Tube to work every day and insists on working full-time. She watches young sales staff come and go, doing their shifts for money and not for the love of the trade. She knows perhaps some of the customers see her as this strange, little old Indian lady who comes to work in her shalwar kameez but it does not bother her.

She knows so much more of the world these young people live in than they think she does. She has lived in different countries, she has seen different things. She has been loved and been broken. She has pieced herself back together again and sought her independence and her own ambition, before girls like Reema were even born. She has made choices that girls like Reema will never know.

Rochan came to see her in the store several times when he returned to London as a married man. He pretended to shop for expensive cutlery, examining knives and forks laid out in oak cases; browsed glass cabinets of sparkling rings and necklaces saying he was looking for a gift for his wife, all the while waiting for a glimpse of her.

He sought her out in Gloves and Leather Goods, begged her to take him back. 'You have your own flat now, we can be lovers, nobody needs to know,' he said.

Shreeya, no longer surprised by his lack of responsibility, met his gaze and reminded him of his wife as well as her own pride. 'We are not children any more,' she said. She walked away.

Shreeya looks at Reema, who has her head down and is making it clear she wishes Shreeya would leave her alone, and pulls a fresh tissue out of the pack that she keeps tucked in the wrist of her cardigan sleeve. She leaves it on the counter, patting Reema's arm.

The morning sales briefing is about to begin and Shreeya wanders off slowly back to Rugs and Cushions at the opposite end of the floor, swaying a little with every footstep like a slow-moving pendulum, her arms held behind her as if she is merely observing and not working at all.

10

In spite of oceans

Sobia, darling!

I can still feel the warmth of your forehead on my lips. For the first time, I have felt that parting can be painful. I may sound silly, but yesterday, before my departure, I wished in my heart that something might happen to delay my flight, like some technical fault or the weather taking a sudden turn for the worse. But it never did. How disappointing! Did you feel the same way?

It has been twenty-three hours since we parted. I don't know how you feel, but I have been feeling terribly, terribly lonely and blue. This flight is monotonous and tiring, as it always is, and I have been constantly thinking about you and our future. At the moment, we are flying somewhere over Romania. The sky is clear and the earth below is clad in snow. I hope it is not the same in London.

Sobia! I must say, you are a very brave girl. I had this fear that you might start crying at the airport but I'm glad you disproved my concern.

Tell me, how did you spend the last twenty-three hours without me? Not as lonely as me, I hope. With God's help, I am hopeful that it won't be too long until we see each other again.

In the meantime, try to keep yourself busy. I'm sure you will find something to do. But if you have any problems, please do not hesitate in telling anyone at home. I'm really pleased that you are adjusting yourself in the new house with Bhabi and Samia baji so well. It gives me a sense of pride and I trust you will keep it up.

Darling! I don't want to stop writing but I am running out of space. Remember me to all. Be good and look after yourself. With lots and lots of love. Yours ever,

Faraz

9th February, 1975
Lahore

My dearest Faraz,

Asalaam-o-alaikum. I hope and pray you reached London safely. How was the long, long journey? The phone rang at 7.15am today and Nabil bhai told us the news of your safe arrival. By the time my letter reaches you, you will have reached home and resumed your duty and must be busy. Did you stay the night in London or did you hire a car from there?

Now, as for me… I have been pretty sad since you left but I have been trying to console myself in some way or the other. I have controlled my emotions quite a lot, but dearest I simply cannot think of being away from you. It makes me very, very sad. My love for you increases with every new day.

You embarrassed me at the airport, kissing my forehead! But anyhow, I enjoyed our parting kiss and your touch.

After we left you at the airport, we came back home and our room seemed to stifle me. I could not stay in it without you, so I went into the kitchen and started helping Samia baji with the cooking. Last night, everyone went to sleep quite early but my sleep was hiding far, far away.

You were in my thoughts and all your sweet talk was ringing in my ears. I will not lie to you darling, I could not control myself then, and I started crying and this is how I fell asleep.

While sleeping, I felt as though you had come back to me and I felt a pat on my back and then I was wide awake again, thinking of you.

Last night there was a heavy downpour of rain with lightning, but this morning it is very clear and there is sunshine. But everything looks so sad to me. Nasreen baji came to me in the morning and I broke down in front of her.

Oh, how far you have gone! I miss you so very much. Every moment of the day, you are before my eyes. I feel I am deeply in love with you.

I also know that in the beginning, I shall feel awfully lonely here with my new family but gradually I shall get used to it. Besides, Bhabi is here and Samia baji and the children, who make me so happy. The children are always talking about you. They miss their uncle. Zafar bhai and Ajmal bhai also ask of your welfare frequently.

But you are not to worry about me. The sadness I feel in my heart is but natural and I am sure you must be feeling sad too. But my dearest, promise me you will not worry. I shall very soon stop feeling so low.

I am keeping busy and the others are looking after me. We all went to Data Darbar in the evening and I saw the golden darwaza. It is marvellous, I must say.

All is fine at home. Everyone sends their love and we all miss your presence. How are you finding work in general practice? And how is the weather there? It must be cold. I wish I could keep on writing but space does not permit it. I shall end now. Reply back very soon as now I shall only want for your letters.

Khuda Hafeez,

With lots and lots of love only for you,

Sobia

xxxx

PS I have been thinking about the immigration procedure. I know the officials can be difficult. Please do the needful with the paperwork and do hurry, as I want to be with you as soon as possible.

23rd February, 1975
Wednesbury

Sobia, darling,

I received your last letter. You can't imagine how thrilled I am to hear from you (or maybe you can). I enjoy every word you write. I go through your letters again and again and visualize you sitting next to me. It is wonderful to be in love with someone, but painful to be apart, isn't it?

I can't blame you for crying like you did. Sweetheart, you are in my heart, in my mind and my thoughts all the time. And of course, in my dreams. Perhaps this is what love does.

Yes, I did stay in London. It wasn't sensible to drive after such a long journey. I have started looking for a house for us to buy but it works out so expensive! Anyway, I have a roof over my head living on top of the surgery.

I have been thinking: perhaps the surgery could be our future abode when you come. It is big, with four bedrooms and a huge lounge, although the kitchen is downstairs which means there is quite a lot of restriction during surgery hours. But living here is not too bad and if we can endure the hardship of staying here for a short while, then we will be able to save some money and buy a new house after you arrive. A small house, but one that we will always cherish.

General practice is entirely different from hospital in many ways. It will take time before I'll be able to adjust myself. I still have to complete my obstetrical requirement. When I'm on call, which is every third night, I have to be available on the phone. That means staying in. It's different from the hospital where you can move around with your bleep and have the company of other doctors.

But on my first night on call as a GP, I had no company, no radio and no TV. I was bored stiff! Oh, I really missed you that night. And you may not like it, but the next day I went out and bought a TV and that too in colour.

The weather here is typically English – dark, wet and gloomy. We hardly had one or two short glimpses of the sun. Some people have envied my recently acquired suntan but I fear I'll gradually lose it.

About your immigration papers: tomorrow I will go to the Notary Public to get the sponsorship forms attested and then I will send them to the Embassy.

Don't be so nervous darling. You are not committing a crime by coming to join your husband abroad. Lots of people have come to England like this. The airport authorities can be awkward and may ask you silly questions but you will be fine. There are many things to sort out but I'll be able to get it done in time.

I think this is the longest letter I have ever written. It is nearly night now. Remember me to all and my love to my little nephews.

Yours ever, with love

Faraz

xxx

19th February, 1975
Islamabad

Faraz Dearest,

Yesterday we left Lahore by railcar and came to Islamabad. We have brought the children to see the snowfall. We are staying with Nasreen baji and I am writing this letter in the same room where we slept when we came to visit before your departure. I feel as though you are here with me, and in a minute, you might walk through the door.

I left Lahore in great anxiety, waiting for your letter. I have only received one letter from you, the one you wrote on the plane, and that too so long ago. You can't imagine how depressed I am when I don't hear from you. All sorts of sad thoughts come to me when your letters don't come. I miss you terribly. Promise me you will write to me regularly.

We went to Muree today. There had been heavy snowfall and it looked beautiful. We stopped the car by the Cecil Hotel and had a picnic lunch and snow fights. Childish of me, I know. I still have not quite got the habits of a married woman in me. I am a bit careless!

Has there been any progress on my sponsorship? A friend of Nasreen baji's came to visit and her sister had been in a similar situation. She said it could take several months for her sister to be granted permission to join her husband in the UK. Sometimes it feels like the Britishers don't want us to be together.

All the others tease me when I am writing to you. So I will leave this now, and write to you again in Lahore. I hope your letters will be waiting there for me. I start each day with hope, but when the postman comes and your letters are still not there, my heart aches and I can only lessen the heaviness by weeping.

All my love,
Sobia
xxx

26th February, 1975
Wednesbury

My sweet darling,

This is in reply to your last letter of 19th February. I feel guilty for not writing to you sooner, but please do not worry when you do not hear from me. The postal service in Pakistan is notorious for its delays. I know being apart is really hard, but there is no need to be anxious. I have been thinking about you all the time.

(2.30pm) I am writing again between patients. It is quiet and I have had time for a short break, some tea, two half-boiled eggs and toast. You know, I have lived alone for years and years and it has not been so bad. But lately I have had this feeling that I am supposed to be sharing it all with someone and that hurts my heart so much. You are so far away, miles and miles away, and I can't share any of this with you except in words. But I keep consoling myself that it won't be long before we are together.

It has been over a month since we married, but it seems as if we have been together for years. Marriage is an incredible revelation, isn't it? Never before have I written letters like this. If someone had told me I was going to, I would have laughed at them. The other day, when I opened your last letter, the surgery receptionist gave me a very big smile indeed.

Your papers are virtually ready but I didn't get the time to go to the Notary Public. But don't worry about the immigration officers. We will talk about it on the phone when I can arrange a call. But remember, you just need to tell them that you have come to join your husband. You don't need to feel shy or hesitant in front of them.

Tell them that you would like eight to twelve weeks entry approval and that you will be approaching the Home Office later for an extension. I also need six copies of your passport photo, please can you send them with your next letter? Oh, and you also need to check your vaccination certificates.

I have been giving some thought as to what you should bring with you when you come. I confess I am confused. It would be nice if you could bring your sewing machine, as you mentioned before I left, but it may be too heavy. In which case, we can buy you one over here when we can afford it. Bring your trousers and tops, but only a few saris and shalwar kameez. You won't believe me now, but you'll soon give them up altogether once you are here. Very few Pakistani and Indian women wear them here, or so it appears.

I must go as I have an afternoon of patients lined up. My dear: each day brings me closer to you in spite of the distance between us. In my heart, I pray for our happiness and everlasting love. Remember once I asked you, do you think people ever get tired of each other? I'm now firmly beginning to believe they don't. We have found happiness in each other.

Bundles of love,

Faraz

xxx

27th February, 1975
Lahore

My dearest,

I have come back to Lahore and still have not received your letters. Faraz, what's the matter? Please write soon. I am so worried and all sorts of sad thoughts come to me. Please give me news of your welfare. Will you do that, dear? I have written a number of letters to you and I wonder if they have reached you. I hope they have.

Now: some big news for you. Congratulations to you, my darling. Yes! It is what you think.

I was not feeling well in Islambad and was running a temperature. Nasreen baji took me with her to the hospital for her own appointment and I took the opportunity to see the gynecologist because I thought I might be expecting, and she confirmed it.

Are you happy? It's a bit early, don't you think? But I am fine. I don't feel anything yet, only that I feel weak in the morning. I have started taking vitamins every day.

I feel so shy that some of the others already know. Samia baji and Bhabi guessed I was in the family way straight away. I went so red. Thank God Abujee is not aware of it! How will I face it when he comes to know!

I wish I could have given you this happy news in person but... now I can think of our baby as well as you. Whenever I feel lonely I will think of both of you. Do pray for me and for our newcomer. I do hope and pray your letters arrive soon.

All my love,

Sobia xxx

12th March, 1975
Wednesbury

My sweet darling,

I don't know how to express myself. The moment I read your last letter; well, it is just the greatest news that I have ever had. I have never felt such fantastic feelings of so much joy and excitement. Darling, I am thrilled. So thrilled. It is a dream coming true! I can't believe it! And yes, it might be a bit early and a little unplanned, but I'm not bothered by that. One has to make a start sooner or later, and we have made it. Don't worry, everything will be okay. Carry on taking your vitamins and iron tablets. Doctor's orders!

As for your shyness, I think you should simply stand on a table and say, 'Everybody! I am going to be a mother!' I am sure Abujee will be very happy to hear the news. He may be a little bit angry with me for spoiling your plans to do a PhD in England, but perhaps you can tell him this is our PhD.

Darling, believe me I have written to you. The Pakistani postal system must be going through some upheaval. Surely my letters are piled up somewhere. I was shocked to hear you have not received any.

Nothing else to report from here. I need your passport photos for your papers. I do hope you can send them soon so we can hurry the process up.

Look after yourself.

Tons of love, yours forever

Faraz

xxx

27th March, 1975
Wednesbury

Hello darling!

I have been looking forward to hearing from you. I hope you received my last letter. I was hoping to see one from you too this morning but I am disappointed. I'm sure there is one on the way. I just suddenly had this urge to write to you and talk to you although there is nothing particularly new to share from my end.

I hope you are keeping well. I can't help worrying about you because I have not heard from you in a fortnight. Do let me know about your welfare.

There was one practical piece of information I wanted to let you know: I have now received your sponsorship papers from the Embassy. I shall send them immediately after this note to you in a separate large envelope. If you get another copy from the Embassy, ignore it. I shall begin organizing your ticket to join me soon. How wonderful!

How are you? I hope fit and well! Do look after yourself darling! Remember me to all at home and lots of love to my nephews and nieces.

It is snowing heavily here, and settling thick on the ground.

I'm okay, but will be better when I hear from you.

With love, yours forever

Faraz

xxx

23rd March, 1975

Lahore

My dearest Faraz darling!

I finally received your letters! I was really very happy to go through them all. Your letters are such a comfort and I feel so joyful after reading them. At first, I used to think love, mohabat, pyaar, or whatever you want to call it, was rubbish and nonsense. But now I realise how true love is. Now that I have heard from you, everything is perfectly fine and I am enjoying life.

Faraz darling! In my last letter, I wrote to you of our happy news. But I need to tell you something else now. I am writing this very calmly, and I want you to be calm too. Please darling, do not worry about what you are about to read. The thought of you being upset makes me very sad. So promise me that first that. Promise? Okay. That's better.

Well, last time I had given you some exciting news but today the news is sad. It is why I have not been able to write to you sooner. In brief, I returned from Nasreen baji's to Lahore and took a bath that evening. While saying my prayers, I suddenly felt very, very weak, stiff and heavy. I found some spotting. Over the Saturday and Sunday I was examined by the doctor and spent the whole weekend waiting for all sorts of tests and results but by then the bleeding was in full flow. I am so sorry to have to tell you this news.

Darling, I had never felt such severe pain before but now I am perfectly fine. Please do not worry. I was a bit sad at the thought of losing the soul inside me and I did feel a bit hollow, but then I thanked God for everything he has given me. What he gives, we accept, and what he takes, we also accept. Darling, if there were no ups and downs in life, it would be so monotonous. So we must face life and reality boldly. So please don't get upset. Yes, we had made a start but it didn't finish; we have plenty of time. We can make another start and pray it ends the right way. That is all we can do.

So now, cheer up and give me a sweet smile. And here's a special kiss for you. As I write to you, there is a sheet of clouds in the sky and sweet soothing breezes passing by the window. This morning was beautiful. See? Everything is fine.

Everyone at home is keeping well. I have started speaking Punjabi with Bhabi and Samia baji but it is still easier for me to speak in Urdu. Poor, poor tongue of mine. It's finding Punjabi very difficult! I will now take leave.

Please don't be upset. I want you to remain happy, okay?

With lots of love and blessings,

Sobia

xxx

1st April, 1975
Wednesbury

My sweetest,

Saturday was my lucky day as it brought my letter from you. I was so relieved to hear from you. I know now that my anxiety over the last few weeks was genuine. Perhaps you won't believe me, but I could sense your distress and I knew something was wrong when I did not receive your letters for so long. I had wanted so very much to call you when your letter finally arrived, but I still do not have my personal line and I did not feel that it was right to use the surgery phone for an international call. I will call as soon as my line is working.

Darling! It is all very disappointing. But if this is the way it is destined to be, then so be it. Rest assured, I have taken it very calmly. You are more precious to me than anything else in the world and it's your welfare that I will always be worried about. It is a relief to read that you are up and about now. Gosh! I can't think of what agony you might have been in. Oh! How I wished to be near you to hold your hands and kiss you.

(Continued on 2 April) I had to stop writing last night because I had to go and see a patient. It is 1am now, and I can't sleep. I have been thinking about you and about us and about our future and thinking an endless chain of thoughts.

My head is heavy. You know what, I think we should take a break in June and get away from all this dull English weather. We will spend a fortnight somewhere sunny, a late honeymoon I suppose.

But now, back to reality. I suppose you must have received your sponsorship forms now. Nabil and some of the others have pointed out that the authorities could be quite awkward and will say that you are using an eight or twelve week entry as an excuse to stay for good. I suppose the answer to that would be to say you are recently married and obviously you want to join your husband. If the Home Office should refuse an extension, then at least you will have a return ticket. But I so hope everything will be alright.

The weekend went quickly. Nabil and I drove out into the countryside. It was beautiful there, hilly and snowy. Wished you were there.

Look after yourself darling,

With lots and lots of love,

Yours ever

Faraz

11th April, 1975
Wednesbury

Sobia, darling!

It was wonderful to talk to you on Saturday. I didn't want to put the receiver down. I hope I was able to make myself understood but I am not very sure – although I could hear you clearly, I had to really shout loud at my end.

By now you will have received the registration letter and all the sponsorship papers. I will need photostat copies of all the forms once you have filled them in, including the pink form from the Embassy. I have already taken copies of my initial request to the immigration officer and the letter with the date of your interview on it.

I know this has all been disappointing because it is now April, and you are still not here. I thought it would be so easy for you to come on a visitor stay but a friend of mine here, a chap called Mubashir, told me it can be quite risky. Mubashir told me that his cousin's wife arrived on a visitor entry but was deported after two weeks. I spoke to Nabil, and he has made enquiries and found a solicitor for me to talk to who apparently has dealt with similar problems.

I called the solicitor and he assured me that there is nothing illegal in you applying for visitor entry but he said he would like to see all the papers we have filled in. I have made an appointment with him next month and hope by then I will have received your completed copies. He suggested that we should not book your ticket or make plans to travel here until he has seen everything.

Darling! I know this news will upset you a lot. But I do not want to take the risk of you being deported after you arrive.

Sometimes, I am so disillusioned by the way things work here that I think about moving away. Maybe we could go to Canada or the USA. I miss you so much and can't think of anything else but getting you here. Let us pray it won't take too long.

I have just realised that by now you must have attended Fazal's wedding. I hope you enjoyed it. I wonder what you wore.

I had better stop now.

Yours ever,

Faraz x

7th April, 1975
Lahore

Faraz, darling

Assalaam-o-alaikum. I was overjoyed to speak to you on the phone. I couldn't believe my ears when I heard your sweet voice after so long. I was so happy.

But at the same time, I am disappointed. It is taking so long to get this sorted.

After we spoke, I discussed the possibilities of me coming to you with Zafar bhai and Ajmal bhai. We all had one idea which was that I could travel on my old passport under my maiden name, and say the purpose of my visit is to meet Nabil bhai. Then Nabil bhai could sponsor me as a blood relative and then later, once I am in, we could work things out. Is this less risky? If so, then ask Nabil bhai to send me sponsorship papers as soon as he can. You already have my passport photos.

It has been three months since we married but we have been apart for so long, and the time is passing so slowly. Really my darling, I can't think of living apart any more. How much longer must we wait? Three months ago we were hardly acquainted but now my soul has changed. My soul is part of you.

Anyhow, I have been busy spending the whole morning packing up one of the suitcases to ship. I have sent my woollies, warm clothes, a few saris, handbags, shoes and photo albums. There is a shalwar for you and a bottle of coffee, I do hope you will like it. And one other gift, a surprise from me. The men who are organising the shipping shall phone you, now that you have your personal line, and then tell you from where you should collect the case.

Fazal's wedding was wonderful, but we were stiff sitting for hours and hours. I extended our congratulations to the new couple. I wore my purple sari to the Barat and my pink sari on the Walima. It was hot, and with all these heavy clothes on I felt it all the more.

I had better stop now. When can I expect your next call?

God bless you! Lots and lots of love

Yours,

Sobia

xxx

17th April, 1975
Wednesbury

Sobia, darling!

Oh! I knew how upset you would be after my last letter and phone call. It is disappointing, I know, I just want to make sure that your arrival is perfectly legal and that we avoid any problems at the airport.

I have talked to Nabil about applying for your entry as a visitor to see him. We are not sure it is a good idea. These days, immigration are stamping the passport of unmarried Pakistani girls entering the UK and making them declare that they will not marry in the UK. If they do marry, they then will have to leave the country and reapply for entry again. So, I think it will be equally risky for you to travel on your unmarried passport as it will be on your married one.

I have talked to the solicitor again and he again has said that there is nothing illegal in you coming on a visitor visa to see your husband. I am seeing him soon and I will ring you once I have done. Please don't forget to send me the photostat documents. Try not to be anxious.

I am glad to hear you enjoyed the wedding. I was trying to visualise you in your fancy saris. I am sure you looked terrific as ever, but perhaps more relaxed than on our wedding day! I will always remember how you looked when you came to me that day, and how I looked like a comic with that hat on. Sweet memories!

Sobia! I realise how lonely you must feel without me. Darling! We miss each other equally, but for now at least this is the way our lives are destined to be. We are interwoven. But please do not look backwards or be sad. We are moving forwards towards a glorious future. Gosh, look at me. I have become terribly romantic, don't you think?

I must stop now. Weather is dreadful. It's cold, windy and hardly any sunshine. There have been several snowy days.

Remember me to all.

Yours ever more,

Faraz xxxxxx

27th April, 1975
Lahore

Dearest Faraz darling!

I pray this finds you in the best of everything. I have received your letters today and, finally, the sponsorship forms. I have given the photostat copies to Zafar bhai and asked him to post them to you. I hope you receive them before seeing the solicitor. Best of luck! I pray your trip will be successful and will bring us some brighter hope and then we can make a new start.

Yesterday, a friend of Bhabi's joined us for tea. She also told me that her cousin was deported from the airport too when she arrived in London. Poor girl, she couldn't even meet her husband. She is now in Iran and will be coming back to Pakistan soon. I shall talk to this girl and get more information from her when she is back.

Gosh! These Britishers are quite harsh, aren't they? Ajmal bhai came up with an interesting suggestion. He said not to buy a return ticket, so that if they tell me to go back, I can say I don't have a ticket. So then they will have to send me back at their own expense! How amusing!

This week has been a very busy one. On Saturday, all the girls came and we had a lot of fun. We sang songs and listened to music and really enjoyed ourselves. At about 2am, it came to an end. I have taped all the songs we sang as I know you will enjoy them. Yesterday, we invited all the near relatives for lunch. It was a very pleasant day. I have taken some family snaps and will send you them when they come out.

A friend of Zafar bhai's, Fazal Mahmood, came to visit. He was very nice. He has offered to take some of my things with him to England – he says he has two empty suitcases I can fill. So I shall pack them with heavy bulky things like coats and bedspreads so that when I come myself, I can travel light. A lot of people have been giving us different gifts too but I do not know if I can bring it all.

Today, we went to attend Iffat baji's daughter's wedding. Uff! I have had enough of these weddings and having to wear such heavy, heavy clothes. But then I must do as the elders say. I don't even want to wear all the gold jewellery but then they keep saying I have to because I am still a new bride. I have had enough!

Darling, please don't regret going to England. I know you feel lonely and disillusioned with the process, but when we are together we will finally feel rooted. Though we may be apart physically, we are together in our thoughts, always. I think about you all the time and pray God grants us the peace of being together very soon.

Things are starting to get very expensive here. The price of sugar, ghee and flour have all shot up. There's been a lot of strikes and processions and people have started criticising Bhutto's party quite openly.

It is very late now darling, so please grant me permission to end and I'll meet you in my dreams.

With all my prayers and love,

Sobia xxx

4th May, 1975
Wednesbury

Sobia darling,

I am terribly lagging behind in writing to you. It was a delight to speak to you again last night and hear your voice from miles away. I hope you were not disappointed by our talk.

Darling! You do realize that I want you here, but I do not want to take the risk that you might get sent away again. So we must wait.

I don't know if you could hear me properly over the phone, but as I said, I have been to see the solicitor and he says airport immigration is getting stricter. He is writing to the Home Office here and to the British Embassy in Islamabad, requesting for a visa for you. It may take three weeks before we get an answer.

I also went to see the Immigration Advisory Bureau, which is a government organisation which helps Asian immigrants with these kinds of problems, but unfortunately they did not have any straightforward answers. I have been advised to write directly to Alex Lyon, Home Minister. I will write to him if all else fails.

Whatever is destined will happen. I want you to be with me so that we can start our life together. At times I am frustrated, and I start thinking about the States or Canada, but I haven't done anything officially yet.

I shall collect the luggage which has been sent. But I would rather have you than your suitcases, darling! Was it not possible for you to squeeze into one?

I suppose the marriage season must be over by now. Yes! It is indeed difficult that you can't dress the way you like to just because you happen to be a newlywed. I think you should start a movement – 'Freedom to Dress' – how's that?

The weather is getting warmer and beautiful at last. There is a cherry tree in the garden which is beginning to blossom. Last weekend, I was not on call so I took Nabil and Saleem (a friend you have not met) to Warwick Castle and Stratford-upon-Avon (the birthplace of Shakespeare). It was quite enjoyable. How I wished you were with me!

I think I should stop now because the cleaning lady is going out and I can give her this letter to post. Remember me to all, and look after yourself darling.

With lots of love,

Faraz

xxx

15th May, 1975
Wednesbury

Sobia darling,

I have not yet received any letters from you. There is nothing much new to share, but I suddenly felt the urge to drop you a line. I am feeling quite homesick, my better half not being with me.

The solicitor has not made much progress yet. In the meantime, I'm drafting a letter to my local MP. The strange thing is that we have not had an MP for quite a number of months. Our MP, a certain Mr Stonehouse, went to the States and disappeared from his hotel. He was thought to have drowned in the sea, but then they discovered millions of pounds missing from odd funds. He was finally traced and arrested in Australia on a forged passport. To cut the long story short, because of some silly British convention, Mr Stonehouse could not be sacked and remains a member of parliament! However, we have had another MP covering his absence and I managed to find his details without too much difficulty. I hope he proves to be helpful.

The good news is that the government has approved a pay rise of 38% to GPs. This means I'll get roughly £1,200 to £1,500 more pay. It is a great relief. I will start looking seriously for a house but there is still the problem of raising the deposit, which will be easily over £1,000.

I am not working this weekend, so will spend some time doing domestic work. The fridge needs defrosting, my shirts need ironing and all the linen must be washed. Aren't you impressed by the things I do, darling!

I will stop here because Nabil and his landlord are coming for dinner so I will be busy later doing the cooking. I have bought a pressure cooker, so let's see how it works. My last cooking experiments were rather nasty so I hope it will be better this time! We are planning to see a movie afterwards – Earthquake. I have heard it is very good.

Yours ever with love,

Faraz xxx

20th May, 1975
Wednesbury

My sweet darling,

I think the hot summer in Lahore is making you lazy! I waited for your letter again this morning but was disappointed. The Pakistani postal system really is tiresome. I will continue writing and I will try to call until your letters start arriving here. I do not know what is happening to the post at your end.

I have been working all weekend but have been bored to death in the evening on my own. Nabil has gone to London. I wish so much you were here.

How are Zafar bhai and Bhabi and the children?

I have heard from the local MP. His letter was a typical politician's response – non-committal. But he is at least writing to the British Embassy in Islamabad. My solicitor is also writing to them. It's all terribly, terribly frustrating and disappointing, darling, but we must keep on trying.

I am thinking of taking a couple of weeks off and flying back to you. I often have some crazy ideas, like maybe you and I could meet somewhere on the Continent and spend a few weeks there together, and then you fly back to Lahore and I fly back to the UK. How do you like that idea?

By the way, I'm really beginning to feel proud of my cooking. I cooked kitcheree the other day. It was a bit gritty, I don't know why, and the rice was out of proportion, but other than that it wasn't too bad.

I'll stop now, I am longing to be with you. You give me strength and a purpose in life. I'm mighty, mighty proud of you and will always be. You are handling things so well in Lahore. This will all be over soon, so don't you worry, okay?

I think I'll stop now, it is past midnight.

With love and yours ever,

Faraz

xxxx

15th June, 1975
Wednesbury

Good news at last darling!

Today I heard from the MP again and he has received a letter from the British Embassy in Islamabad saying that they will consider you for a priority visa, provided we can send them evidence that this is our first marriage. The solicitor has our marriage certificate from our Nikkah and will send it to them. Let us hope for a quick and favourable reply. I suppose they may write to you and request you to come for an interview sometime soon. So do look out for that.

In the meantime, my application for British citizenship has been approved, and that too may have some bearing on your visa.

I have finally been to collect your luggage. I have folded all your clothes, neatly, into the wardrobe. Don't worry about your tops being too short. It is the fashion anyway, and I suppose you must have heard of a girl called Twiggy. By the way, I found my gift from you. I held it for ages; a souvenir from my beloved wife!

You said on the phone that you had forgotten my face! How could you do that! It will be most interesting if you fail to recognise me when we meet again. You know what I will do? I will give you the longest kiss in the world and then you will know it is me. How about that?

The weather is beautiful. This is the hottest June since 1950. I have a strong feeling about everything.

With lots and lots of love and happiness – there may not be much longer to wait now.

Yours ever,

Faraz

xxx

27th June, 1975
Lahore

My dearest, dearest darling!

I am awfully sorry for being so late in writing. When I realised my letters weren't reaching you, I stopped for a while. I am so sorry. When I arrived home last night, a few of your letters had piled up for me while I had been away. I was so pleased to see them. I hope you have got my letters that I wrote from Islamabad by now, but it does not sound like it.

We have spoken on the phone, even though it has been brief. But now they are saying the postal delays are clearing up so I am writing to you once more.

I have returned from a pleasant stay with Nasreen baji and Abujee in Islamabad. It was busy, with plenty of guests coming to meet me while I was there, and while I was away I didn't have much time to write again. I really wanted to write to you last night when I came back to Lahore, but it was nearly midnight by the time I had finished unpacking.

We went to Tarbela Dam while I was away. It was beautiful. It rained in the afternoon which made everything all the more green and there was a cool breeze all the while. We packed a picnic with us and came back late at night. A group of us went, and we had such fun. We sang songs, climbed hills – and even killed a snake on the way back! The weather in the north was much more pleasant than in Lahore. This is the first summer I have spent in Lahore, and it is true what they say about the heat. I am not used to it, having spent summers in air-conditioned houses. But would you believe, in Islamabad, we slept under blankets as it was quite chilly at night.

I am feeling all sorts of different emotions. On the one hand, my trip to Islamabad was a pleasant distraction. But on the other hand, I worry about how long it will be until I can see you again.

I have been meaning to tell you some good news of sorts. Nasreen baji has a friend whose cousin works at the British Embassy. The cousin came to meet me, and said he could help us. He said he pursued a similar case for another friend and his wife, and this woman is now finally off to England. I really pray that something will happen. I don't know how much more we shall have to wait. Sometimes I get so irritated and start wishing we could escape to another world where there are no countries keeping us apart and we could finally be together.

Do let me know what the MP has written to the Embassy so I can let Nasreen baji's contact know. I will go back up to Islamabad next month to see him.

All my love,

Sobia

xxx

10th July, 1975
Lahore

My dearest,

I write to you with great disappointment. I had always thought that I would be with you in a month or two but I have returned from Islamabad and spoken at length with Nasreen baji's friend's cousin in the Embassy. He has asked for more documents – your bank slips, a copy of the letter sent by the MP, a letter confirming your British citizenship, a photostat of your passport. Once the Embassy receives all of this, then I shall be given a priority date for an interview with the immigration officer here. But the interview date will be six months from when the documents are submitted. Six months! Will we even be together on our first wedding anniversary? I don't know. How sad!

Abujee has been consoling me. He will write to you also. I know you will be as disappointed. I have tried hard to control my tears, because tears will not help us. In fact, when I felt them pouring into my eyes, I swallowed them up, summoned my will-power and prayed to God. It is going to be difficult but we will get through this.

Today I read an article in the newspaper: 'Canada clamps down on foreign doctors.' It seems all the countries are discouraging Indians and Pakistanis. Is this what it is like in the UK too?

Nasreen baji and the children were a great distraction from all this. We went to Swat and stayed in a guest house opposite a stream. We took picnics out with us every day. The children were fascinated by the fast flowing water and all day long I could hear the soothing sound of it. We also stopped in Peshawar and met with old college friends.

It was wonderful weather and I had such good company but I still felt so lonely without you. Do you know, it has been six months since we married!

Right, I shall end now. I am getting quite tired after my long journey back to Lahore.

May God always protect you,

With all my love,

Sobia xxx

18th July, 1975
Wednesbury

Dearest darling,

It has been one of those lucky mornings, because your last two letters arrived today. I also had a letter from the Foreign Office. It included a copy of a letter written by Mr Osborne of the Islamabad immigration office. Your date of interview has finally been confirmed – 19 November 1975. Exactly four months from today.

I hope you have received your letter from them too. Four months! It is obviously not going to be easy, but we have survived so long apart already that I am sure we can wait another few months. But I wonder if Nasreen baji's friend's cousin at the Embassy could bring the date forward at all? I will be anxiously waiting to hear what he says. In any case, I think I shall order your ticket from the PIA office.

I have enclosed an article from the Times about the criticism the Home Office has come under for its procedure concerning entry for Indian and Pakistani wives. It has given me some hope that the chances of you being sent back will be remote. I have sent the same clipping to Abujee too.

I am so glad that you have had pleasant diversions in Swat and Pesh. Gosh! You make me envious. I haven't done anything special lately! Life is not very exciting without you. I am keeping myself busy reading books, mainly thrillers. I miss you a lot these days.

How is everything in Lahore? I suppose the monsoons have started. Are you enjoying the mangoes? Do think of me when you are having them. It is not that you can't get them here (they cost 35p each, that's nearly 7 rupees a mango!) it is just that when I think of these things, and you all on your picnics, I feel sort of homesick and miss everyone.

Forever yours,

Love

Faraz

x

5th August, 1975
Wednesbury

Darling,

It is 1am and I can't sleep. It is hot and humid – would you believe it was 84 degrees today. I just felt like writing to you and secondly, I have been thinking a lot about whether or not you should try to move your interview date forward.

There was an item on the television news today, saying that the courts are not changing their stance towards Pakistani wives, since Pakistan is not in the Commonwealth. So I think perhaps there is no point in pushing your interview date forward and we should just wait until November.

I have booked you an open ticket with PIA. It is valid for a year. So at least we have done that.

A friend of mine has been to Pakistan and back. He got married last month and his wife has an interview for December already!

Lucky them. They will not have to wait as long as us. I still haven't received my new British passport but hope to have it this month.

I have missed you a lot recently. The weather has been beautiful and I have been eating chilled plums picked from the tree in the garden with cream.

It won't be long until our ordeal ends. These days, I try not to look at the calendar but subconsciously I am always counting the days.

I'll stop now. Don't worry about anything darling.

Yours ever,

Faraz

xxx

12th August, 1975

Lahore

My very dearest,

It was so nice getting your letters last night. Our postman is ill and his replacement is very inefficient and brings the mail according to his own sweet will. At last, I received a few of your letters piled up together and I feel as though you are very near to me.

Another friend of Nasreen baji's has her interview with the Embassy in October, so I will have a better idea of what to expect then. In the meantime, I shall just wait and keep busy in other ways.

Nasreen baji and kids have been staying with us in Lahore and we are having a fabulous time. The past few days had been very hot and humid but suddenly it has got beautiful and fresh outside. Today, we ate tikkas and hot samosas in the shade of the garden. Later we are invited for tea at Salma baji's house. The children are all fine. We miss you terribly. I have been remembering you every time we have mangos! Ramadan starts soon. Will you fast?

I will try to pick my ticket up this week. I am impatiently waiting for the time to pass and am always looking ahead. Don't you feel like time is passing so slowly? When you left in February, I had never imagined that we would be apart for so long.

Darling, I love you.

Yours ever,

Sobia

xxx

30th August, 1975
Wednesbury

Sobia darling,

I suddenly felt like writing to you. Another month is nearly over and there are still weeks and weeks before us. At least we have your interview date now. But just think! If all goes well, then maybe you will be here by the end of the year.

There are so many things I would like to do, but I keep putting them off until you come. I have been reading classics again. Wuthering Heights is a beautiful book, isn't it? A few years ago, I went past the Brontë family house but it was closed. Perhaps we can visit it together.

Around this time last year, I had only just started to think of you occasionally. That was when Nabil suggested we might make a good pair. And now look! Love sure is a funny thing. You only really know it when you experience it.

I am sure you are looking forward to Ramadan. As for me, I'm one of the baddies who keeps the sanctity but not the fast. Do you know what, you have reminded me about Eid. For years, I had completely forgotten Eid, it was just another day for me. The last time I really enjoyed it was in 1972 when I was still in Lahore. But this should have been our first Eid together as a married couple. And I will miss you a lot. Never mind, we can celebrate Christmas together! Now how's that?

Did I tell you that I am learning French? I have signed up for evening classes. Let's see how much I will be able to learn. Perhaps we can go to Paris for a late honeymoon after all.

Showers of kisses to you,

Yours, Faraz

(A word of advice — try not to accept any Eid gifts like dinner sets as we simply will not use them here.)

14th September, 1975

Lahore

My dearest darling,

I hope this letter finds you in good health as we are here. The time doesn't seem to pass in Ramadan. There is so little to do. The days are more and more monotonous. Sometimes, I feel we women in Pakistan have such useless lives. What use are we, if we are not able to do anything? What to do with these old traditions which say we should stay within the four walls of the house only?

Seeing as I am unable to do much in Ramadan, I have been reading the Quran and, do you know, I was quite ignorant of religion before but now I am beginning to learn more. Sometimes I get your letters before we break our fast and your words serve as an excellent appetiser.

Not long to go until my interview! I am feeling a little anxious about it but have been praying earnestly that things will go in our favour. I wish, wish, wish that I could come to you straight after it.

The other day I read an interesting piece in the news, saying that Pakistani wives wanting British citizenship would have to remarry in the UK. Honestly! The stupid laws of that country make me angry. Anyhow, I think the Embassy has everything from us so now we shall just wait for the interview. It is a hell of a lot of work to come to the UK, isn't it? Do you face this sort of hardship all the time?

I don't know. I just don't think I will have the courage or the stamina to wait much longer to join you.

Even though we have never been together on Eid before, I feel like I will miss you more than anything this Eid. How I wish we might celebrate Christmas together instead! What would we do, I wonder?

Sweet dreams! Missing you ever so much!

Sobia xxx

(Yes! Wuthering Heights was a good book but I prefer Charlotte over Emily!)

9th October, 1975
Wednesbury

My dearest lonesome!

I knew how you would feel on Eid and I hope you are back to your normal cheerful self after missing me. I felt the same. Life must be back to usual now, no?

I have not had any letters from you for about two weeks. It is very unlike you but I suppose the post office must be slow because of Ramadan and Eid. I am not worried or annoyed at all, it is just that your letters are so much a part of my routine and I kind of feel incomplete without them. Maybe there will be a letter soon. Your letters make my day, sweetheart!

Darling! It won't be long until we can stop our letters and I can plaster you in kisses.

I am sure everything will go well at the interview. Your anxiety is natural. But you must realise that the British immigration officers are by nature awkward. They may well ask you silly and irrelevant questions. But don't be hesitant or shy. You have a right to come here.

I have heard that the immigration officers sometimes ask to see personal correspondence between couples. They might want to see our letters. It seems unethical but I suppose the British Immigration Department is beyond ethics. You are within your rights to refuse to show them our letters. I know of someone who refused, and the officer did not ask her to show her letters again.

Time is passing slowly. The evenings are getting dark and frosty (you will get used to them!) and the surgery is packed with patients who have the flu. I am trying to get our abode into a presentable shape for you but no matter what I do, my untidy habits leave it looking the same.

Must stop now.

Yours with love,

Faraz

xxxx

P.S. Do check your vaccinations before your interview. You'll require cholera, typhoid and small pox.

19th November, 1975
Islamabad

Faraz darling!

You must have got my telegram. I am writing to you from Nasreen baji's as we have just entered the door from our trip to the Embassy.

Oh, I am so happy! I cannot express my joy. We shall be together! I can't explain how it felt when they handed over my passport with the visa stamped on it.

I was called in for my interview at midday, but spent an age waiting. Oh! How difficult those moments were. I prayed inwardly to God that it would all go okay. In the interview room, they gave me more forms to complete – asking me things like your name, my in-laws' names – and watched as I filled them in. And then the immigration officer turned to me and said, 'Well, in light of all of the correspondence which I have before me, I don't think I will have to interview you. You will get your visa today and you will be able to join your husband soon.'

I was so shocked and thanked him and came out, I couldn't quite believe it. After so many months, that was it. So simple!

Darling, our worries are over. Now I shall be able to come and join you, my jaan. We will walk through life together. You have become so close to me, there have been times I felt like the distance between us had disappeared and we were together already. We shall be together for our first wedding anniversary! And perhaps Christmas too!

All my love, forever,

Sobia

xxxxxxxxx

25th November, 1975
Wednesbury

Darling!

Yes! Finally the tension and suspense is over! I did not realise it would be so simple. It must have been because of the MP's letter and the other correspondence. And I suppose the immigration officer could find no reason to hold back on your visa.

How I wish you could fly to me today! Do you think you could get here in December, before the end of the year?

There is something I wanted to surprise you with but I will tell you now. I have applied for a mortgage and with good luck, we shall have our own house by February! It is a small house, neatly tended, and it will be just right for us to start our new chapter together.

The weather is getting extremely cold now, but don't worry darling. My love is warm enough!

Faraz

xxx

14th December, 1975
Wednesbury

Sobia darling,

There is hardly anything to write, except that in exactly one week from now, you shall be here and that is the most comforting feeling! But time is still passing awfully slowly and so I have thought to pick up my pen and write one more time.

I presume you are very busy with packing. We must speak on the phone before you leave so that I may have some idea of whether all your luggage will fit in my car. My guess is you will exceed the permissible limits, so please try and cut it down to the essentials. Perhaps leave behind the glittering wedding clothes and jewellery that you do not care much for anyway! I will leave home at 6 or 7am in order to reach London in time, but if I am late, don't panic. Just wait in the arrival lounge. But of course, I will do everything I can to reach you on time.

Our wait is finally over!

I shall save my kisses for you in person!

All my love,

Faraz

xxx

23rd December, 1975
Lahore

My sweetest, dearest love,

This shall be my last letter to you before I arrive. I have not much to say except that when I think of our meeting again after such a long, long time, my heart beats louder.

On the one hand, I am quite sad to leave all my loved ones behind but on the other hand, I am so glad to finally be in your arms! I shall feel so safe and secure with you by my side.

I can't wait to see you. I can't wait for our life together to start.

Sobia

xxxxxx

About the author

Huma Qureshi was born in the West Midlands to Pakistani parents. She graduated from the University of Warwick in 2003 and worked as a journalist for the *Guardian* and the *Observer* for several years before becoming a freelance writer. She lives in north London with her husband and son. *In Spite of Oceans:Migrant Voices* is her first book.